The Running Body

# The Running Body

A memoir

by Emily Pifer

AUTUMN
HOUSE PRESS

*Pittsburgh*

THE RUNNING BODY
*An Autumn House Book*

ISBN: 978-1-637680-54-4
LCCN: 2022938585

Autumn House Press receives state arts funding support through a grant from the Pennsylvania Council on the Arts, a state agency funded by the Commonwealth of Pennsylvania, and the National Endowment for the Arts, a federal agency.

AUTHOR PHOTO: Rose Curtis
COVER & BOOK DESIGN: Kinsley Stocum

*for my parents*

# CONTENTS

# I.

EVEN THOUGH I knew the process of its making, I could not stop staring. Could not stop touching. Could not stop asking: What am I becoming? Looking in the mirror was like looking at a sculpture and wondering how it could have possibly been made from what was once a different thing entirely. Flesh wrapped tight around muscle around bone. Every rib self-evident. Tendons so exposed. There were all these parts of me I had never seen. I called the sum of these parts the running body.

The crater in the center of my chest felt like a kind of becoming. I remember the first time I saw it in the mirror—so deep. I took a step back then forward then pressed two fingers inside of it and felt a twinge of ecstasy then checked to see if the purple V-neck I planned to wear to the movies that night would cover it. I knew it was alarming because seeing it there in the mirror alarmed me, even though I'd been waiting for it, measuring its depth daily.

A few years earlier, in a high school English class, we read about Narcissus, the immaculately beautiful son of a river god and a nymph. The first time he saw his image reflected back to him from a pool of water, he became eternally, tragically rapt in what he saw blinking back. I often had trouble with, or was troubled by, or have trouble with, or am troubled by the question of truth in Greek mythology. Some of the so-called myths rang (ring) terribly true to me.

IT'S NO LONGER that summer, but sometimes it's always *that summer*, that summer between my freshman track season and sophomore cross country season at Ohio University, that summer the running consumed me, that summer when beginnings blurred into endings, that summer I became running body. Early that June, before the crater appeared, my teammate Juli and I flew with Chris, our assistant coach at the time, from Ohio to Oregon for the Junior National Track and Field Meet. I had never been so far west, had never been on a plane. At Hayward Field in Eugene, I ran a personal record in the 5K, but I don't remember my exact time or place or anything else about the race. Instead, my memories from the week I was in Eugene consist mostly of images of thin, hard running bodies. I spent most of that week looking at professional runners whose heights and weights I knew as well as, if not better than, their accolades. I looked and looked and looked as they leaned towards National Champion titles, World Qualifying times, American records. Juli spent most of her time looking, too. She'd say things like, "Her abs are crazy," and I'd nod, never knowing exactly which particular athlete she was talking about.

After finishing first and second in the National Championship 10K, Shalane Flanagan and Kara Goucher, the two running bodies on which I fixed my gaze most closely, jogged easy around the eighth lane—skin and muscle and smiling. I stood along the fence and watched the sun set on their sharp contours with two issues of *Runner's World* magazine pressed to my chest. When I held the one with Shalane on the cover out to her, she grinned down at the image of her body, then she popped out her sharp, spandex-covered hip and rested one hand on it, pointing her other hand toward her image on the magazine. She looked up to me, grinning, and said, "Who's this hottie?" As she took my pen and started signing, I wanted to stop time and tape measure all of her dimensions and compare them to all of mine.

But I don't want to mislead. It's not as if Shalane handed the magazine back, my hands replacing hers, and just like that, it was decided: The running body would soon be all that was left of me. For a long time, I'd been calculating, measuring, testing, burning.

When I was a real little girl, must have been four or five, I would dive and flip and slide and cannonball and arms-up-scream into the kidney bean-shaped pool that gleamed in the backyard of our ranch house on Meadow Wood Lane in Scott Depot, West Virginia. I would hug my knees and laugh and laugh as my dad threw me like a beach ball, from the shallow end to the deep. In the air I would spread my arms like wings. After a brief moment of flying, I would land with a smack and a splash and when I resurfaced, I would still be laughing. I would ask him to do it again and again, rapt by what he could do to my body with his body.

When I was a little older—seven, eight, nine—I went through a period of touching very hot things. For instance, the red-hot ring on the stove top would call to me. I would reach out and pet it like a puppy. Then, I would be screaming, my hand already swelling and blistering. "Why did you touch that?" my parents would always ask me, but my answer was always unsatisfactory: I wanted to know what it felt like.

Around this time, I started playing basketball. I hated it, and I hated practice—so many opportunities to do the wrong thing—but I loved the sprints we did at the end. Our coach called them "suicides." At the end of each, instead of slowing and stopping at the black perimeter line, I would throw my body as hard as I could into the mats a few steps beyond it. The mats were blue, and when I threw my body against them, I liked how everything else turned blue too.

Soon after, I joined the swim team. It quickly proved to be a better sport for me because, unlike basketball and softball (which I also tried), swimming did not generate stomach-ulcer anxiety, shaped by the pressure to contribute in clear and measurable ways to a team, the fact of the ball coming at my body, the fact of my body not knowing what to do with the ball. On the swim team I specialized in breaststroke. Pull, kick, glide, breathe. Pull kick gliiiiiiiide breathe. Together, the pull and kick ask a question: Water, will you hold me? The glide delivers its answer: Yes, yes, completely. Getting out of the pool at the end of practice, I was always shocked at the weight of me. In the water, body weight is reimagined. The result is a womb-like feeling, which I preferred over nearly all others.

Then, in late elementary school or early middle school—I can't remember which—there were three projects that seem to foreshadow my future proclivities. The first was a trifold poster on the Bermuda Triangle. The second was a trifold poster on cults.

The third was a short story called "Against Her Will," which cul-minated in ten pages of evening-news paranoia. In the story, the unnamed protagonist is abducted from her bed while home sick from school, her parents both at work. She is then chained up like a dog and sexually assaulted. Eventually, she escapes out of a win-dow inside a Chuck E. Cheese bathroom, finds the highway, and hitches a ride home with a trucker who helps her return to her "old life." After the protagonist helps the cops arrest her kidnappers, everything settles down and goes back to normal very quickly, and at the end, she feels as if she is supposed to go back to normal too. But how could she? She doesn't know, cannot say. Together, these three projects seem to engage a duality with which I am still reckoning: the fear of losing my will to choose what I do with my body, the longing to be released from that particular driver's seat. There's both a terror and a comfort in knowing there are places you can never come back from; there are ways to give yourself and your body over to something all consuming.

Later, during the summer before eighth grade, a new friend at my new school in central Ohio—a state that, six months before, I cried and said I did not want to move to, on account that it is gray, flat, and boring—had asked if I wanted to join the cross country team. I did not know what she meant by "cross country," but after she explained that it was running through fields and woods as fast as you could, I eagerly agreed. Cross country sounded a lot like swimming—you're part of a team but there's also this sense of being out there on your own, competing against everyone else but especially against yourself, and especially against your muscles tiring and your lungs burning, and of course, my friend assured me there would be no balls flying. At our first summer practice, our coaches, Dr. B and Coach K, instructed everyone, but especially the new runners, to make our runs short and easy, and to walk if we needed to. I joined a few girls for a jog from the high school track to the town pool and back, about a mile and a half. When we stopped at the pool for a drink from the water fountain, I felt a sense of longing.

The next afternoon I went for a run by myself. I must have been chasing that feeling. The heat felt different than it had ever felt before, like it had somehow turned me inside out, leaving my organs to bake. My legs felt one thousand pounds each. My lungs felt on the brink of explosion. At the turnaround point of the three-mile run, out on empty asphalt—gray flat boring, yes, but also sparkling with heat—near our new two-story house, I stopped, pressed my hands to my knees. Eventually, I started stumbling around in the sun. When I began again, with every step I remember thinking: Icannotkeepgoing, Icannotkeepgoing. A mile and a half later though, having somehow kept going, I reached our driveway. The rest of the day, I felt almost haunted by a new experiential knowledge: Pain is a kind of company, a kind of witness, a kind of opening. Pain could be all of these things, and I had made it myself, right there in my body.

Then, by the time I was sixteen, I was saying "I love you too" as my body blundered against the body of another in the front seat of his hand-me-down Ford Explorer. I had no idea what I meant when I told him that I loved him, but I didn't know what else there was to say, and I didn't know what else there was to do. If my body was a tool, I wanted to know its utility. I wanted to find the exact line between what I could and could not do with its machinery.

When I was seventeen, at the end-of-season cross country banquet, Coach K, who'd become a mentor, gave me a copy of John L. Parker Jr.'s cult-classic running novel, *Once a Runner*. I started reading it during the ten-minute car ride home. Later that night I highlighted, "Pride necessarily sprouts and grows; a pride that can only come from relentless kneading of unwilling flesh, painful months of grinding and burning away all that is heavy, all that is strength-sapping and useless to the body as a projectile." As I read, I imagined my body as something different from my body. I imagined it harder and thinner, like the book's protagonist, Quenton Cassidy. I imagined grinding and burning away at flesh I did not realize was unwilling. I felt the edges of low-boiling questions moving closer and closer to the surface of things: How do I purge myself of all that saps my strength, steals my speed? How do I get rid of all this heavy and replace it with something lighter, made for running?

In *Once a Runner*, Cassidy, a college runner, prepares for an upcoming race with a monstrous workout: forty 400-meter repeats, each under 60 seconds per lap, or under a 4-minute pace per mile. On the track and off, Cassidy's focus is brutal and complete. His running body is made from solitude and sacrifice and a hunger for hollowness I recognized somewhere inside me, somewhere I wondered if I could reach.

At the end of each season, Coach K wrote everyone on our team letters. I used mine as a bookmark. "You are the most dedicated athlete I've ever coached," it began. On the backside, I rewrote one of my favorite lines from the book in capital letters: "GAUNT IS BEAUTIFUL."

After finishing *Once a Runner*, I used my lifeguarding money to buy Chris Lear's *Running with the Buffaloes: A Season Inside with Mark Wetmore, Adam Goucher, and the University of Colorado Men's Cross Country Team* at the Barnes and Noble one town over. Holding the book in my hands, gazing at the running bodies on the cover, made me feel nervous and guilty. Somehow, I could feel the book's power, and I knew whatever was inside would be threatening.

In one of the first scenes, Mark Wetmore, the Colorado distance coach whose coaching philosophy is inspired, in part, by Tom Wolfe's *The Electric Kool-Aid Acid Test*, counts the number of exposed ribs on Adam Goucher's torso. It's just after a race that Adam, the team's most promising runner, didn't win. Wetmore pinches skin, tells Adam if he loses five pounds, next year the race will be his. Soon after, Adam decides to stop eating lunch. If he feels like he might pass out before practice, he eats one of those 100-calorie Quaker Chewy bars. How simple, I remember thinking.

Then there was the time, during my first semester at Ohio University, when I realized the first weeks of October passed and my period never came. My boyfriend Aaron and I weren't having sex yet, but I drove to the Walmart in Athens and took a pregnancy test in the bathroom anyway. When the stick showed negative, I felt delusional for thinking I could be growing a whole other life inside me. I didn't get a period the next month either, and that's when I remembered hearing something somewhere about this happening when female athletes overstress their bodies by working too hard and not eating enough. It must have been when the nutritionist visited the seminar that all athletes at the university were required to take. I remembered the term for it and Googled "female athlete triad." Scanning the results, I felt pride about what was, apparently, happening inside my body. I ignored the part about bones weakening; red flags flashed green.

Then, one Friday during the spring before that summer: cherry blossoms, hot sun, cool breeze, classes yawning into a pre-finals lull. The whole campus warming up for play at its strongest sport: partying. It was the two-week window between the end of track season and the beginning of summer training, and I ran both my morning and afternoon runs without eating before or between. It was one of the first times I tried this, and I impressed myself with how long I could run on empty. That night Aaron picked up a pizza, and even though I added a slice to the hollow in my stomach, it still felt cavernous. Before I finished the slice, he mixed me a drink. Captain Morgan and Diet Dr. P. Strong, like I always said I liked it. I blacked out before I finished it, then I finished it, then someone poured me another, probably. Later, a friend held my hair as I bent over the toilet. I came in and out of the blackout as my whole body heaved. Empty, emptied. I woke up on another friend's couch, curled next to Aaron with my clothes on, mouth dry, stomach vacant and rolling with need. I ate one of those hard, crunchy granola bars then went running. It had been a long time since we'd had a weekend like this—without a race or even official practice. Our distance coach Rick had assigned the women's team only six miles at a moderate pace.

I ran with Aaron instead of meeting up with any of my teammates. Our sweat smelled like liquor as we cruised along the bike path and talked about nothing. I felt something like free moving alongside his body. Still, every time we ran together, jealousy and resentment threatened to masticate away at all the good feelings. His body was harder and smoother than mine. He could decide he wanted to pick up the pace at any moment and drop me, my thighs and chest small, practically pubescent, but still bouncing. And what bothered me most is that none of that was because he was better than me—I worked harder, with more focus, placed better amongst women than he did amongst men, showed more promise as an athlete—it was because of his body. Lower body fat and greater muscle strength seemed to mean higher speed over longer distances. I looked over and wished my chest could be as flat and firm as his, barely moving as we curved around the mud-brown water of the Hocking.

When no one I was with the night before seemed to worry or wonder how or why I blacked out so quickly, I knew I was on to something. When, just after our run, one of the fastest guys on Kent State's cross country team, who was partying in Athens that weekend, said something to Aaron about how "fit" I was looking, I knew there were parts of me burning. And when Aaron told me what the Kent State runner said, he looked at me like he had never looked at me before; it felt like eating something very sweet.

I wrote all that so you know, long before I got to Eugene, I'd already become entangled with certain kinds of fantasies, certain kinds of feelings, and I'd already begun making decisions in the hopes that I might pull them closer to me. Decisions like: Run more and more and then more. Eat less. No, less. No, still less. Ignore the warning signs, ignore what your body thinks it needs. Be tough, gritty. Empty your body of what weighs it down. Empty of what you can't use for distance and speed. Run your self out of your body, then you can be free.

What happened in Eugene that summer is I ran out of decisions. The burning up of my body no longer felt up to me. I surrendered.

THAT SUMMER, AFTER returning from Eugene, I read *Running with the Buffaloes* again, this time purposefully searching for strategies to burn and grind and knead. I read and reread every description of the runners' bodies, noting how they seemed to harden and shrink throughout the season. As I read, my mind kept snagging on Adam Goucher's decision to fast from breakfast to dinner, no matter how many miles he had to run that day or how hard his workout was going to test his body. How simple, I thought again. How simple, I kept thinking. Soon, it started to feel romantic—lying under the leisured breeze of the ceiling fan while my body ate itself for lunch.

Somewhere between asleep and awake, I would dream my body on the starting line, sound of bullet ringing, smoke in the air, adrenaline rush and rush and rush as legs floated over terrain, pain and pain and pain, then the other side of pain, the perfect and the nothing. In the dream my body was no longer mine; it belonged to the running. What I mean is the body that was mine had become a body *from* and *for* running. And all the parts of me that were not specifically made for running faster and farther were gone. Just like that—just like *poof*. In the dream the body I was inside was very hard and very fast. And nothing could stop the running body once it had replaced me: It kept going and going.

Late June and it was happening. No longer a dream—I felt each ounce burning. Eighty, eighty-five, ninety miles a week. In the bathroom mirror while brushing my teeth, morning and night,

I touched the places where the body had emptied—convexities between bone, wide openings between thighs and ass cheeks, muscle striation where I did not know muscle could be.

I researched and memorized the BMIs of all the professional and collegiate distance runners whose bodies I yearned to inhabit: Shalane Flanagan, Kara Goucher, Lauren Fleshman, Jordan Hasay, Sally Kipyego, Tirunesh Dibaba, and so many others whose names I never thought would slip from my memory. I thought if my BMI dipped lower than every competitive runner in the country, and then the world, I would have a chance at matching their abilities. I spent hours searching for and staring at images of the fastest long-distance runners in history. I thought it was so beautiful how you could tell just by looking at their bodies that they were made to do the very thing they were doing.

That summer, I taught swim lessons and occupied various lifeguard stands at the Groveport Aquatic Center, just like I did during the seven summers before. Sitting or standing under the sun for eight hours at a time turned out to be the perfect antidote to the call of my hungering. As long as I didn't pack any food to eat during my breaks (which I never did) and stayed away from the snack stand (which I always did), more and more flesh got kneaded away every day. Every morning, after I finished my run, I unwrapped a half-melted PowerBar and ate it in three bites on the way to the pool, peeling off my sports bra and spandex shorts and pulling on my red bathing suit at the long red light on Waterloo.

After my double shifts, I almost always ran again. Usually with Penny, my best friend from high school who ran at the University of South Carolina. When I got home, twelve hours of sweat later, I ate quickly. Vegetables, mostly. A can of tuna dumped on top, maybe. Then, if I felt my body was deserving of dessert, or rather, if it was still shrieking in hunger, I would heat up frozen fruit in the microwave and sweeten it with a few drops of honey.

I can't remember if it was me or Penny who first started blaming our weight loss to one another on the extreme heat and humidity: "It's just too hot to eat." I guess whoever said it first doesn't matter because whichever one of us said it, the other always agreed.

On rare days when I wasn't working, I would step on the scale in my parents' bathroom no less than five times per day—usually many more. I would tiptoe through their room, just like I did as a kid, while they were at work or downstairs watching TV or out on the porch reading. I weighed myself in the morning after I woke up, after my first run, before my second, after breakfast, after dinner, before I went to bed. It quickly became a favorite compulsion—I loved to see and feel and know that I was lessening. It became a game—this shrinking, shrieking body. No matter where I was throughout the day, I maintained as much space as possible between the body and food. If the panging became desperate for mercy, I would mix a packet of lemonade-flavored Crystal Light into my water bottle and make a plate of carrots and pickles to dip in spicy mustard.

One evening, while I was still at the pool readying myself to teach another round of swim lessons, I saw a coworker I hadn't seen since our first session of lessons earlier that morning. "You look even skinnier now than you were last time I saw you," she said. We both looked down at the running body in the red bathing suit. I didn't hear concern in her tone. Instead, I heard curiosity— or even envy. More than anything, it was just normal. It was just the way women always seemed to talk to one another, sizing up each other's bodies. "It's been so humid," I remember saying. "I'm sure it's water weight. I never stop sweating."

There are many ways to measure loss-of-body, and that summer, I became acquainted with all of them. The scale, of course, but also the loosening of clothes and the way Aaron and other guy friends started picking me up and swinging my body around as a greeting, and my favorite of all: looking.

One evening, my dad saw me coming in from a run and asked how much weight I'd lost. I shrugged—trying to hide my fear of getting caught—and he said my legs look lighter, my stride smoother. I'm making running look easy, he said. Does it feel easier for me? "Just be careful," he added, "You don't want to get too skinny."

But I was already climbing the stairs, on my way to inspect the running body in my bedroom's full-length mirror. I wanted to see what he saw when he looked at me—but our mirror image is always a distortion; it's the reverse of reality.

One day while I was watching the people in their big inner tubes float down the lazy river in my red one-piece, which had begun to hang off my body like drapery, an emaciated woman walked up to me.

"People always tell me I'm too skinny, but look at you," she said while looking at the body in its state of becoming and unbecoming. "We're the same!" she shouted wildly. I glanced at her body then looked away quickly. I laughed a little, which is something I still do when I'm not sure what to say but want to seem pleasing; something my mother taught me.

If you're trying to imagine this emaciated woman, try to imagine a woman who vacuumed all but the necessities out of her body, then turned herself inside out, then covered herself back up with skin. I don't mean to sound crude; this is what the woman looked like to me.

Later, after I rotated positions to the top of the slides, this woman ascended the steps with her heavily labored breathing. I gave her the cue that it was her turn to go and she sat down at the top of the steep, straight slide and nudged her bones off until gravity took over. I watched her body blur then crash into the water below.

Later, while I was working at the first-aid station, the woman came up for a Band-Aid. I stayed back in the corner and gathered no details about her injury.

"Doesn't that woman look like some kind of drug addict?" I asked the guard sitting next to me after she walked away slowly.

"Not really," he said. "Just a woman who doesn't eat."

In July of that summer, I flew from Ohio to Colorado to visit Aaron. He was interning at a mountain resort in Estes Park, and we hadn't seen each other since the end of May when he dropped me off at my parents' house after the end of the school year, wrapped his runner arms around me as I leaned against the side of his hatchback, squeezing my torso tighter than usual. Earlier during the drive, he'd said, "I don't think girl runners eat enough." I don't remember the context or my response, only the guilt-burn-caught-in-headlights feeling as it shot up my spine.

On the first day of my Colorado visit, Aaron took me on a short hike that ended at a crystal-clear lake. There, he wrapped his hands around my evaporated waist, his fingers meeting in the middle of my back, and picked me up like we were practicing that routine from *Dirty Dancing*. He'd never picked me up before, but he did it so naturally, as if all that time, he had been wanting and waiting.

Later that evening, after we finished a ten-miler, he picked me up again. His fingers tightened around the emptied-out parts of me and squeezed. "I think you're getting lighter," he said, shaking the running body around like it might dispense money. I wriggled in his arms.

"I don't know," I said when he finally set the body back down. "Maybe."

The next day we ate lunch with some of his coworkers, and on our way to a trail that afternoon, he started telling me about one of the women. Back at lunch I'd noticed this woman because she ate only a carton of diet vanilla yogurt and an apple.

I'd noticed how she sliced the apple very carefully, then dipped it in the carton, giving it a yogurt coating. It seemed artful: a kind of dance. I'd noticed, too, how she labored over each bite, taking breaks between them as if she needed to catch her breath. As she ate her small and careful lunch, and as I ate my entire burrito—the altitude and travel and hard morning run making it impossible for me to ignore my body's panging—I compared our bodies. She was thinner, but I was harder. Her body, unlike mine, was not whittled down by the force of pounding roads and trails under feet. Bringing her up out of the blue, mountain-carved sky, Aaron told me she'd been struggling with an eating disorder for a while, and had been in and out of treatment. Either she'd just been, or she was going back soon, or both, he wasn't sure. I stared out the window while he kept, again and again, looking over at me.

The next morning we ran eleven miles around the Boulder Reservoir. Aaron wasn't feeling well, and for the first time, I went on ahead, cruising smooth and swift in the dry heat. After we both finished, we changed into our bathing suits in the backseat of the car we were borrowing, sweaty hot hard limbs tangling, and spent the afternoon lying under the sun on bath towels, wading into the cool water, constellating around our hardened bodies.

"I can see every muscle in your stomach," Aaron said as we packed up to go. The words came out lightly, awe-filled and curious, childlike, but there was something accusatory in the icy blue of his eyes.

"I can see every muscle in yours too," I said, reaching out, touching.

"That's because I'm a guy," he said, flexing dramatically.

When we woke up on the last morning of my visit and had only a few hours together before it would be time to drive back down to the airport in Denver, Aaron suggested that we skip our run. I agreed there were more important things, so we spent the morning eating blueberry pancakes and breakfast burritos at a small café on the side of a mountain, then we visited an animal sanctuary. Later, as I settled into my seat on the plane, I felt a sense of winning—against what? I could not name it, not quite, but the combination of not running plus big breakfast minus total freak-out made me feel like maybe I was okay after all, like I had a handle on things.

That night, back at my parents' house in Ohio, I unpacked my suitcase, quickly separating the clean from the dirty and filing away unworn socks and tank tops. When I got down to my running shoes, though, a flip switched. Minutes later, I was down in the basement cranking up the treadmill in my underwear while the rest of the house fell asleep. When the machine hit eight miles, just a little before midnight, I slowed to a walking pace, sweat-drenched and relieved.

Eight hours later, I was ten miles into a thirteen-mile-long run when I realized I had taken a wrong turn out on some back roads I'd never run before. I'd found my way back to familiar roads but was still miles from my car when my GPS watch buzzed to report that I hit mile eighteen. My stomach was knotted and empty, plus, I knew Rick would probably scold me if I told him about this run—he never wanted us to run more than fifteen miles at a time, but I could never remember why, or I could, but didn't care, so let it slip through my mind. After quickly sorting through the pros and cons, I stopped my watch and started walking. Dried-up salt stuck all over my skin, and inches of space spread between my spandex shorts and thighs. Eventually, I walked by the Catholic church where I was confirmed, where I used to sit in the pews and stare at the back of my high school boyfriend's head, where all those people tried to get me to believe in something other than the sanctity of a road empty save for a body running, legs churning while the heart pumps and pumps, everything circulating.

The parking lot was a third of the way full; there were dozens of variations of the same SUV. I imagined all those cookie-cutter-looking families keeping to themselves in their pews, the men with their arms stretched out along the polished and curved backsides, the babies staring and drooling and giggling and whining, the children playing with small toys or their faces, the teenagers thinking way more about sex than Jesus—all the real Jesus-loving teens went to those big churches with the light shows and the electric guitars and the preacher in tight pants and the dancing—and the mothers making mental grocery lists, laundry lists, shit lists. I imagined all of those people kidding themselves or trying to kid themselves into believing that faith is a replacement for knowing.

Sometimes that summer, before falling asleep, as I laid awake counting, measuring, spiraling, as my leg muscles twitched and tingled in uneasy relief, I worried I had gone too far, needed help, a way out. The longer I stayed awake the more desperate my spinning became. I wondered if I would ever again be able to eat without thinking about eating less, or run without thinking about running more. I wondered how I slipped into the grip of something that felt so much stronger and more powerful than me; that felt somehow, impossibly, both outside of me and *of* me. I spun through my day. The obsessive dedication to push-ups: before and after both runs, on my break at the pool, while waiting for the shower water to heat up, right before bed. The way I ran for miles without having a single thought—like my mind wasn't there at all. The strange knowledge that had been established between time and distance and the running body. I could often leave my watch in the car, take off and trust that whenever I returned, I would have run for nearly the exact amount of time and miles I set out to.

I often felt empowered and in control during the day, but in the dark, it was as if a veil was lifted and I could suddenly see the way all my thoughts, actions, and desires were infested with delusion, dangerous and multiplying. By the time I woke up, all I could ever think about was running. All I wanted to do was pull a sports bra over my head and go deeper into the thing.

August in Ohio always means hot wet heat, but that summer was particularly sauna-like. Coach K and Dr. B invited me and Penny and a few of the other recent graduates to join the high school cross country team on their annual retreat. Back then, I looked at nearly all of those high school runners and saw a lack of drive and focus—I found it off-putting—but I hoped that me being there would show them the kind of runner that they too could be. (Now, I hope that none of them have any memory of me.)

Back in the parking lot at the end of the weekend, after most of the runners were gone, Dr. B, an older man with a large belly and crisp white hair, walked slowly towards me. "You've lost so much weight," he said, speaking softly. "People who have seen you around town running stop and ask me if you've gotten sick." His fuzzy white eyebrows crinkled in concern as his pale blue eyes drilled down into the running body. "Are you sick?" he asked.

One hundred alarm clocks went off in my bloodstream. Out of instinct, I had been avoiding him all weekend, but now he had pinned me. I told him I was not sick. I told him our coaches just had us doing a lot of running. I told him I was eating a lot—a whole, whole lot. I smiled very big, too big, maybe, then closed my lips over my teeth.

Within days, three men I barely knew looked at me and told me what they thought I should eat.

"You should eat a cheeseburger."

"When's the last time you ate a cheeseburger?"

"Eat a cheeseburger."

I smiled and told them all I ate more than they'd think.

I went to one of those grocery-store clinics to get a round of school-required vaccines. The nurse said, "Now give me that little bird wing," as he stuck a needle in the arm of the running body.

Instead of watching the needle go in or the blood come out, I watched my mom: She was beaming.

My mother swears she's been troubled by the body all her life, and I insist this isn't true. Not because I don't believe it, but because I don't want to. She tells me a story her mother must have told her: At one of her first checkups as a baby, my mom's mom, my Grandma Sue, picked up the baby that became my mom and tried to lower her baby body on the scale, but the baby kicked her feet into the air, shrieking and shrieking.

My mom says she knows what she was doing. She says, even then, so small, she didn't want to face her own weight. I insist this is coincidence because I want it to be.

"It only makes a good story," I tell her, "but there's no way you could have known what was happening."

"I think I knew," she tells me, laughing the laugh she gave me.

I must have been very young when I realized my mother's beauty. So young I can't remember it now: the instant her beauty came into focus while so much else stayed blurry. People would ask me and my brother and sister rhetorical questions like: "Your mom is so beautiful, isn't she?" But despite her beauty, my mom has always had a difficult and complicated relationship with her body. As a quiet child bent toward surveillance and eavesdropping, I became a quick study in the subject of my mother and her body trouble, troubles, troubling. It seemed that while everyone else agreed in regard to her beauty, she called her arms chubby and her face too round for this or that hairstyle, and any time a camera was pulled out of a purse or pocket, she put her hand in front of her face and insisted, "Not right now." When she did this, though, it's important for you to know that she embodied the glamour of Jackie O, trying to preserve herself from the greed of the paparazzi.

As a kid, I'd tiptoe into my parents' bathroom to open the top drawer on my mom's side of the vanity. I'd wonder over all her little tubes and tubs filled with various potions and promises to enhance beauty while fighting, combating, going to war against "signs of aging," that most cursed and menacing enemy. When I was a little older, I'd roll my eyes at the supermarket as she'd steer our cart to the altar of candy-hued products. She'd pick up and put down a handful of different promises before choosing. I'd complain I was tired, thirsty, hungry. She'd squint at each of their labels. Shift her weight. Sigh, feign carelessness, then toss her careful choice into our cart and say, "Ready?" I'd always try to move close to the register as we were checking out. I wanted to see what it cost.

When I was only a few years old, my sister Molly, who is thirteen months older than me, and I moved with our parents to the ranch house on Meadow Wood Lane. In the kidney bean-shaped pool in the backyard, Molly and I quickly learned to swim, dive, flip, slide. My younger brother Isaac came along soon after, and he became a water-baby too. We spent all summer in our bathing suits. Molly and I played made-up games like "Titanic," which was mostly about trying to crawl up the faded-blue slippery slide while someone else pulled on your leg and you screamed that you were drowning, and "The Sixteen-Year-Old Game," in which you pretended like you were sixteen.

Our babysitter Whitney was in high school and blonde and lived across the street where she had clothes like D. J. from *Full House* and a tanning bed. Out at our pool, she always wore one-piece bathing suits. One afternoon, as we balanced Styrofoam plates filled with boiled hot dogs and potato chips on our laps, she said she was feeling fat. My little voice in response was both empathetic and matter-of-fact: "Oh, don't worry about that." I took my small tanned hand and placed it on her chest, like I was trying to feel her heartbeat, then I brushed it right over and down past her breasts, watching it float in the air above her ribs and stomach. "You're not fat until this part sticks out more than this part," I said, pointing towards her chest, then her stomach: "See."

Whitney and Stacy, our other blonde, suntanned, thin teenage neighbor, would come over in the evenings sometimes just to use the pool. I liked to sit on the side with my feet in while they treaded water for as long as they could. As they moved their legs in and out and round and round, they'd adopt the same look on their faces as my mom did when she mirrored her body's movements to those of the hip-bearing ladies in her aerobics videos. It was a kind of flushness of the cheeks, a set of the jaw, and an effort in the eyes I would soon associate with the relief of punishing one's body. I understood that their in and out and round and round was some sort of calorie-concerned activity.

During one summer towards the end of elementary school, my best friend Maggie moved into an apartment complex just outside of our neighborhood. Her family was building a new house farther away, but for a few months, there were only a few minutes of walking or roller-blading between our bedrooms. So often it was: sun-warmed legs and feet clacking down the big, steep hill at the entrance of Meadow Wood in my peach-colored jellies, walking up the three steps to her door, giving the bell a ring, and asking, "Can Maggie come out and play with me?"

Maggie put butter on her Pop-Tarts, to the horror of my mother, and then, of course, the horror of me. Her soft belly stuck out of T-shirts and those tankini bathing suits we were all wearing. We were so young, but I'd already learned so much about how to see difference, how to see bodies.

In our basement, my favorite thing to do was to give Maggie makeovers. "Can we play the makeover game?" I'd ask, and when she agreed, I'd take out my mom's old makeup and smear it on her face. One day I painted clear nail polish with gold glitter flakes all over her eyelids. I was saying, "You're going to look so pretty," as she started to scream.

As the end of that summer got closer, the high school football team's early morning practices started colliding with my morning workouts on the track. "See that, boys?" the high school football coach shouted to a line of padded players across the field one morning, his voice carrying to the running body as it floated around a curve, easily working through a three-mile warmup. "That's called zero body fat," the coach continued, "that's what working your goddamn ass off looks like, boys."

I sat in the front of this man's class all through sophomore history. As he shouted, it felt like I was watching the running body glide over ground from the perspective of all those teenage boys he was telling to watch me. I saw the limbs smooth and effortless, saw the body that was once mine crossing an invisible line between dream and reality. Each step was an offering. Or a proposition: Please consume me. From this perspective, I saw everything flowing and fluid. The running body kept circling the track and the field and all the other players and coaches, adding an extra mile and drills and strides to the warmup. I never wanted to stop looking at the running body through the lenses of the boys being told to look at me.

Soon after, I saw a group of friends from our men's cross country team. One said, "Pife, you're wasting away." Another picked me up in the middle of the street. "Oh my God, you weigh nothing," he said as he swung me around like the running body was a dog toy and the other guys were hungry puppies. Another called me a monster. I smiled because I knew he meant it in a good way. I used to tell myself no one ever said anything, but now I know I was either not listening or not understanding or both. Deep into that summer and throughout the fall cross country season, men often tried to get me to eat. Even when they praised my body—"see that boys?"—or asked me questions—"how did you get so lean?"— their words felt snagged with unease. I sensed their worry—"you should eat a cheeseburger"—but even their concern felt affirming. Any commentary in regard to the running body or its ability became something like food: It kept me going.

It was different with women, though. No matter what their responses were in reality, I always walked away thinking: She wants to look like me.

August burned away to September, and every day of that summer: deeper into the thing. I went back to Athens for our preseason training camp and twisted my teammates' concerned looks into jealousy. I could not or did not distinguish delusion from reality. Their stares were encouraging. Their disapproval proved it was all working.

I cried in my closest friend and teammate Melissa's car after one of our first practices back with the team, but neither one of us addressed what was actually happening, I just knew the older girls were talking about me—I felt it the way you can always feel those things, that energy. But what were they saying? I didn't ask, and Melissa didn't tell me. Instead, she held me, two pairs of razor-edged shoulder bones shaking. This is how I know truth is heavy—in the car that day, I felt it sink to the bottom, felt us both learning how to tread and float and glide right over it.

When, soon after, a few of the guys on the men's team started mimicking what Juli and I ate for dinner at the dining hall—we usually skipped all the hot-food lines and constructed very large salads with lots of toppings—I thought that meant it was all working; I thought that meant I was going to get away with what I was doing to my body.

One morning, around this time, our graduate assistant coach asked if he could run with me after we finished our morning lifting. We were a half mile in, September sun steady rising, when the small talk faded and I felt his words coming the way you can smell winter coming.

"Some of the girls are concerned with your weight. I just want to make sure everything's okay. And that you're, you know, eating and stuff," he said.

More alarms, more ringing. The running body stiffened its stride. I could not think of what to say, but the words came anyway.

"They shouldn't be worried about me," I said. "They should be worried about Juli."

A few miles later, he mentioned a few new lifts he wanted to implement into our team's training. "It's the kind of stuff," he said, "that will help the other girls with their weight too."

At the end of our summer training camp there was always a big party. When I was an incoming freshman, this party dangled out in front of me, tantalizing. No one was supposed to drink the week beforehand—which seemed like a big deal to a lot of people on the team, but made no difference to me since I was not yet drinking regularly and had never drank at all until my junior year of high school. That night my friends Carly and Molly and I waited all night to grab neon-colored wine coolers from Carly's mom's fridge and sneak them back up to her bedroom, trying not to let the bottles clank together as we blundered our way through the dark. We drank fast while watching TV, and at some point, my stomach got so full of snacks and liquid that I puked when I started laughing and couldn't stop. Everything that came up from my stomach looked like it was dyed with red ink. I think I was drunk on the thrill of our transgression, not the sugary booze. By my senior year, my friends and I started drinking more—plastic-bottle vodka mixed into orange juice or Sprite—but even then, it was always special, always marking something. Back then I didn't know that alcohol itself could be both the mark and the something.

We'd heard the preseason party would be only runners at first, but as the night got rolling, football players and wrestlers and the swim team were likely to show up. We'd heard the big, old, falling-apart Victorian house where most of the older guys on the team lived—affectionately called The Vic—would be totally destroyed that next morning. We'd heard Mark the Landlord would show up to check on things, fuming. We'd also heard the first part of the night was reserved for team-building activities—the freshman girls would be separate from the freshman boys. No one ever said the word "hazing," but we understood that the lines would get blurry. I'd bought a short, tight, cheaply made, strapless dress just for the occasion.

In the damp basement of an apartment shared by a few of the older-girl runners, the other freshman-girl runners and I were given a cooler of beers and an iPod that could dock into a small set of speakers. We were told to choose a song from the iPod and to choreograph a dance that we would perform at the party—in the backyard, once it got real packed and real dark out and everyone could gather around and hang out the upstairs windows and they could turn the floodlights on our bodies. Someone chose a Rihanna song about being a rockstar, and with most of our small group buzzing with adrenaline and alcohol, we got to work.

One of the junior guys elected himself to mix Melissa and me extra-strong vodka cranberries as soon as we arrived at the party. As we sipped our drinks, I remember feeling like all the wound up parts of me loosened up and for once I was untangled and flattened out. When it was finally time for us to get out there in the grass and do our dance, Juli never showed up. Afterward, we heard she fled the scene right as the music started playing. One of the upperclasswomen walked her back to Boyd Hall. I don't know if I hit all the moves or stayed on beat, but I remember how good it felt to know that everyone was watching. I didn't know how to leave so I stayed until morning.

At that time, I was still dating Adam, a nice guy a couple of years older than me. He was a junior at Ohio State, over an hour away, and though I'd tried to break up with him before leaving for

Athens, I never tried hard enough. The morning after the party I felt relieved: I didn't remember everything that happened, but I remembered kissing Aaron outside of Boyd, under the harsh fluorescent light. It must have been at least three. When I called Adam to confess my transgression, he said that he would be willing to work on things. I told him I felt too guilty and that I could never forgive myself, even if he could. After I hung up the phone, I felt free. Free, I suppose, to keep making out with Aaron.

Walking into the dining hall the afternoon after the party to join the rest of the team for brunch, I remember feeling like I was part of something, even if that something was getting drunk and doing drunk-person things, or maybe, especially because that something was getting drunk and doing drunk-person things.

A year later, I would think of that girl, walking into the dining hall feeling hot and triumphant and freed, as incredibly stupid and incredibly silly. A year later, in the middle of the same preseason party at The Vic, I would lock the bathroom door and weigh the running body. I would stare at the numbers until they became blurry. I would stand in front of the dirty mirror and watch my face swallow plastic-bottle vodka from the red cup in my hand, and I would feel that the person I was gazing at was somehow both no relation to me and also the exact person I was meant to be. The rest of the night I would feel like I was observing the running body from outside of it, dressed in tight dark skinny jeans and a tight black tank top, sports bra and GPS-watch tan lines making geometric patterns on skin. I yearned to step outside of that body for real, to survey every inch of the work in 3D. By the second time I went to the bathroom to pee, after I had swallowed the rest of the terrible drink, I stared at the running body and could not keep from thinking: It's complete.

"Are you sure you're okay?" asked Rachel, a friend from high school, when she stopped by the house on her way to another party.

"I think she looks like a Victoria's Secret model," Rachel's friend Allie answered for me.

I smiled and insisted that I was fine. With Aaron in earshot, I suggested we leave the party and walk uptown for pizza. I dipped both of my oily slices into deep pools of ranch. I ate like I was performing because I was. In the morning, I woke up early and ran for over two hours with Juli.

"... WITH JULI."
"... with Juli."
"... with Juli."

After we returned to school in the fall, this became my running log's refrain. An epistrophe at the end of so many entries. Our entwinement became a fact peeking through all my fictions.

"Hilly dogs plus eight by ten-second strides on the football field with Juli."
"Fifteen mile long run with Juli."
"First street hill repeats, stayed with Juli."
"45 minutes in the weight room after practice with Juli."
"Rick canceled the long run. Eight miles easy with Juli."
"Flat dudes plus bike path for ten with Juli."
"Four miles around the Ridges with Juli."
"An hour of yoga after practice with Juli."

We both came back from that summer burned away and burning. We became silent partners in crimes against our bodies. I wrote poems about us moving along the routes we called Rick's Ten (which was actually eleven miles), Angel Ridge, Long Point. I wrote about how we were divided, but by the same things—the same needs. I printed the poems out and read them to her before I handed them in for Introduction to Poetry.

Juli wrote in her running log like it was the kind of diary

with a lock and key. Really, it was just one of those black-and-white composition books that Rick bought in bulk and handed out one by one to everyone on our team, but she filled it with the kind of language you make for only yourself to see. She documented her anguish and anxiety. Detailed her aches and pains and doom. She was making history—not just story—out of her body.

Across the hallway, I did things differently. I covered my composition book with stickers that said things like "USA Track and Field" and "Running Freak." I took it everywhere with me. I curated and calculated with the painstaking care of someone conspiring how they'll flee a crime scene after they commit the crime that creates the scene. I knew Rick would ask for my log at the end of each season, just like he did with Juli's and Melissa's and the other top runners before us, studying to see where we went wrong and right and in which directions we should keep pushing our bodies, and so I only included the details I wanted him to see, and how, of course, I wanted him to see them. Nothing like Juli's straight and narrow lettering, mine was slanted and dodgy. Fiction, really. Magical realism, maybe. Every sentence played defense, anticipating evidence that could be raised against me. I replaced space—empty and blank—with shields to reality.

What do these differences mean? Maybe it's simply that Juli is a more honest person than me, but I also think she wanted something from Rick that he never offered and perhaps could not afford to give (i.e., help). I think, at the least, she wanted him to know what was happening—what she could not help but keep doing to her body (i.e., starving).

On Thursday nights that fall, I went over to The Vic to eat dinner with Aaron. He loved to cook and eat, and because I knew I would have less control over what I would consume at his house than I did when I ate dinner at the dining hall, on Thursdays, I tried to eat even less than usual throughout the day. On Thursdays, I tried to eat nothing.

After dinner one night, we watched *When Harry Met Sally* at my request. We had to try hard not to fall asleep after double workouts and classes and studying. It had only been an hour since roasted pork and mashed potatoes and broccoli, but my stomach was loud and angry. I saw a granola bar on Aaron's nightstand and on impulse, reached. "Can I have this?" I asked as I peeled back the silver wrapping. Right before I took a bite, I realized it was one of those Quaker Chewy bars with the hard, caloric brown chocolate shell surrounding the sticky oats. I knew it added at least 50 calories to the original Quaker Chocolate Chip Chewy's 100-calorie promise. "Actually, I'm not hungry," I said, placing the opened bar back on the nightstand. From here, a duel began.

"I don't know. I'm just not."

"I know it won't make me gain weight."

"I'm just not hungry anymore."

Aaron asked if I was sure four more times before he gave up and ate it for me. When we kissed after, the taste of chocolate on his lips was menacing.

In an ice-cold tub of water, Kara Goucher sits between Adam Goucher's legs. At the time, they were both running professionally for Nike. The video is called "Eat a Dorito," and it was published to FloTrack, a popular site for running-related content. Kara's voice shakes a little as her body shivers. She holds her shirt up against her chest. Adam isn't wearing one. And even as I watched the video over and over again in an attempt to work against my disordered mind and the body that reflected and refracted it, sometimes I couldn't help but focus mostly on the deep striation in their stomachs, the exposed veins of their necks, their running bodies.

Kara starts by talking about the beginning of her time running cross country at the University of Colorado, and the beginning of her relationship with Adam. Then she tells the story of Adam inviting her over to his apartment for dinner. She'd ran twice that day and had eaten only a PowerBar, she says. She showed up to Adam's apartment the way I so often showed up to Aaron's: very hungry. But Adam didn't have dinner waiting like she hungered all day expecting. He didn't even have the ingredients he needed, and he told her they'd have to go grocery shopping. She says she was so hungry and shocked that tears pooled in her eyes. Adam popped open a bag of Doritos. "Eat a Dorito," he said. She said she was fine, she'd wait. "Eat a Dorito," he repeated and repeated—easily recognizing what was happening because of his own experience with starving. "Eat a Dorito. Eat a Dorito. Eat a Dorito," he kept saying. She broke down, she says, cried to Adam, told him that she'd dug herself into a dark hole, and that she needed help being pulled out. Every time, I cringed at this part of the story. I knew I would never let myself cry out for help to Aaron. Besides, he always had dinner ready.

One afternoon that fall, a pack of runners from the men's team moved toward the running body across a part of campus we called East Green. "Hey, Little Kara!" one of them called. I beamed and fell in stride with their bodies.

In late September, an issue of *Runner's World* got passed around the bus on the way to a meet. Melissa was on her laptop, legs stretched out on the row of seats across from me. Most of my other teammates were doing homework too, and most of the men's team was asleep in the back. Our coaches and athletic trainer sat up front. The overhead space up there was always filled with apples and bananas, granola bars and little tubs that held a single serving of peanut butter, water bottles and Gatorade. When someone passed the magazine to me, it was already flipped to the story everyone had been reading and talking about. "How Megan Goethals Got Her Groove Back," reported by a former University of Michigan runner named Rachel Sturtz, follows Megan Goethals' path from very fast middle school runner to very fast high school runner to very fast college runner to very broken and very sick and in treatment for an eating disorder she'd had for nearly as long as she'd been running. Apparently, she didn't know she'd been starving for years. I slouched down low in the seat as I read.

The first time I ran against Megan was in high school. It was an invite-only meet, featuring the fastest high school runners from Indiana, Ohio, and Michigan. Back then, I was shocked when she beat me. I thought she looked sick. Back then, I had never seen a runner as thin as Megan was. I didn't yet know the way her extreme thinness would begin to look normal or nearly normal to me—that bodies like hers populate every NCAA starting line. By the time I was running in college, when I would see her at meets, I would still think she looked sick, but I would also think she looked fast. That mythological line between sick and fast had gone blurry—so blurry I started to question whether it existed at all.

I felt scared and anxious and defensive reading Megan's story. I recognized what I was doing to my body, what Juli was doing to her body. I wondered if this was what most of us, from the front of the pack to the back, were doing to our bodies. At the same time, I recognized stark contrasts between Megan and me, and these differences in our stories, and in our bodies, enabled me to create distance between what happened to her and what was happening to me. First of all, Megan got diagnosed and treated for anorexia. She was hospitalized and forced to eat. According to her doctors, if she hadn't stopped running and started eating more, she could have died. Second of all, nearly everyone close to her—coaches, teammates, family—and far away—people posting on popular running-related message boards, especially—named what they thought she was doing to her body (starving) and urged or even demanded that she get help. *No one has ever forced me to eat*, I thought to myself while looking up from the magazine, out the window at gray Midwestern skies and bean fields and nothing.

The article ends on a hopeful and triumphant note, citing how much Megan eats now and how fast she's been running. After the magazine rotated through most of our team, someone brought up the article and we all said the same sort of things.

"It's so sad."

"She's so crazy!"

"I'm glad she got help."

"I always knew there was something wrong with her. She looked so scary!"

For the rest of the drive, I tried to shake Megan's story out of me. I closed my eyes and visualized: running body on starting line, gun raised, ready.

In November, Juli became the Mid-American Conference champion, and I placed seventh. Two weeks later, I raced poorly at the NCAA Regional meet, my legs as heavy as boulders, and didn't even come close to qualifying to race in the National Championship. Juli had a breakout race and two weeks later at Nationals, she became an All-American. That day, Melissa and I ran around the championship course in Terre Haute, Indiana. We screamed and danced and cried for Juli. We curled our arms around her, we smiled for photographs, we chatted excitedly with her excited family. I felt the painful irony that you can be both happy for someone else and sad for yourself. I was more than sad, though, as I smiled for photographs and clinked wineglasses during Juli's celebratory meal—I hated myself for failing. I seethed, just under the surface. *Juli is an All-American, and I am nothing.* The thought played in my head on repeat.

Soon after Juli's All-American performance, at our family Thanksgiving at my grandparents' house in West Virginia, my dad's younger brother, who I hadn't seen since before I burned down to the running body, told me he was glad to see that I put some weight back on. His mouth was turned down and his eyes told a story to which I was not privy. Because I knew that he had not seen me for many months, and that he never saw me *before* I gained a few pounds back after the cross country season ended, and that this was in fact the lowest weight he had ever seen my body at, his comment meant that my dad must have been talking to him about me and my body trouble, troubles, troubling.

My mind flashed to the weeks before, when I went home to visit my parents after the conference championship. I said something small about not being very hungry for dinner after having a large lunch. "You're eating dinner," my dad had said, stern and quiet, though somehow booming.

I nodded my head in response to my uncle. I smiled, small and weak. I was (am) always trying to placate and appease. I wondered, though, what else I had been missing. Who else had been talking? Were people worried about me? The questions did not stay with me long, though. Instead, I spent the rest of the evening in crisis negotiations with myself: It's okay—good, even!—that you let a few pounds back on in the off-season. It's nothing that can't be fixed.

That winter was mostly cold and dark and my hunger was desperate and unending and I could not discipline it. I was back at my grandparents' house for Christmas dinner the first time it happened. Rows of baked meat, casseroles, cakes, pies, cookies, nut mixes, and sweet tea lined the kitchen. Before that night there were visits to the dining hall where I lost control—could not stop eating. And there were times when Olivia, my roommate and close friend from the track team, was working late at the art studio, and her large bag of trail mix would catch my eye, or my eye would catch it, then I would be jamming handfuls into my mouth. My hands would always try to do as much damage as they could before my mind intervened.

At my grandparents' house though, the intensity of my hunger became desperate and without end. I ate for hours straight. I kept going back to fill my plate. If my mom left a bite or two of pie on hers, it would absolutely torture me until I either ate it for her or left the room. Either no one noticed the amount of food I was eating because I kept moving from kitchen to dining room to living room, or no one said anything to me. I knew my dad's oldest brother was far more likely to comment on my sister's consumption of one slice of cake than he was to comment on the fact that I had been compulsively moving back and forth between the main meal and the sweets. As the hours passed and I struggled to take back jurisdiction over my mind and body, I sat in the small back room where my grandma kept winter coats and collars and leashes for dogs long dead and does the laundry. There in the small back room, I played games with a small cousin at a small table. There was a large plastic jar of peanuts, Chex Mix, and M&M's in front of me and I was scooping them into my mouth. I felt detached from the whole scene—like I was watching it all go down from afar, or maybe on TV, either way, helpless to interrupt my body's great need. It felt like a rebellion was happening inside me. Even though my stomach felt like it might explode, there was also an unsolvable emptiness. I considered asking my small cousin for help. It hit me suddenly: I wanted to tell her everything. And I wanted to ask her if I looked fat, or if I looked skinny, or what she thought of my body. Do I look like a runner? Do I look fit and fast? Do I look like an All-American? I know I am taller, but am I thinner and harder than Juli? But I knew my small cousin did not know Juli. Did not know what an All-American looked like. And above all else, could not help me.

I spent the weeks between Thanksgiving and New Year's working at the large indoor-outdoor mall about thirty minutes from my parents' house, up the highway. I folded clothes in that particular Abercrombie & Fitch way—or, I tried, often giving up and scrunching the tank top stack until it, somehow, masqueraded as

46

"on brand." I walked around aimlessly in the near-dark, trying to look busy and trying to hear something new and something interesting in Mariah Carey's rendition of "All I Want for Christmas Is You," which played no less than ten times per four-hour shift. I stood outside the store and practically shouted at mall-goers as they entered. "Hey! How's it going?" I said, a wide smile stretching across my face. I was playing Homecoming Queen pep mashed against East Coast prep, and I somehow felt more honest like that than I did when I was just playing myself. At least as I walked around the mall on my breaks in my dark blue, skintight Abercrombie jeans, brown leather flip-flops (in often freezing weather), plaid button-up shirt, and navy cardigan, everyone knew I was playing a part. And that this body they saw was part of the whole transaction—I smile at you *like* I've been dying to see you for weeks, I ask how you're doing *like* I genuinely care, and you pay them then they pay me.

Getting the job felt like winning something. It was near the end of that summer when a woman stopped me while I was walking through the mall, asked if I'd ever thought about being an Abercrombie model. At first I thought she meant *actually* modeling, but it turns out they call all their in-store employees "models." I knew the whole thing was totally and disgustingly superficial. I'd heard stories about this happening to many of the popular girls at my high school. I knew not just anyone could be an A&F "model" (I knew you had to be conventionally thin and pretty), even if all being an A&F model meant was unlocking dressing rooms doors and helping confused upper-middle-class mothers understand the concept of ripped jeans you buy that way. But despite countless trips to the mall during high school, blowing shameful chunks of my lifeguarding money with Penny, no one ever stopped to ask me if I wanted to work at Abercrombie. I supposed I didn't yet have the right look—that I wasn't thin enough yet. And even though I made less wandering around those densely cologned rooms than I would have teaching swim lessons or lifeguarding at the indoor pool, and the drive was much longer, and the discount wasn't good, and even if it was, I didn't actually like the clothes—even through all of that, I worked there because it was validating. Self-awareness was not enough to reason with the parts of me that needed to squeeze my little flattened ass into those skinny jeans more than I needed almost anything.

The food court quickly became troublesome, though. I pictured it there in the middle of the mall during my shifts. I lusted for it. All those smells. All those gleaming signs. All those people eating like they were not scared to eat. They ate like they were not even thinking about eating, just doing it. Like they were not ashamed or guilty. Sometimes, after my shift was over, I could not refuse the parts of me that were screaming and clawing toward the counters. Sometimes I would buy big pretzels dripping with butter and sugar and thick blonde brownies. Sometimes I would buy something then throw it away before I could finish it, so that I wouldn't finish it. Usually, when I let my body go at it in there— impossibly bright lights and voices chattering in shopper's high—I stopped at the gym on my way home. I would pull on my one-piece and swim laps, then strap on a water-jogging belt and make big circles in the deep end until the pool closed. To pass the time, I would pretend I was being interviewed by a running magazine. I would detail the past season's disappointments, all the struggles I had faced. I would tell an underdog story. I would imagine a future where I was a National Champion or an Olympian or both. Back in the locker room, I was always shocked by how thin I still appeared. I looked pale and fragile—like you could see through me, like I might break. I still resembled the running body, even though I could feel it slipping. I stepped on the scale and held my breath. I promised myself I wouldn't lose control again.

When the roads got too snowy or icy, I'd cranked out miles on the treadmill in my parent's basement. On the wall beside the machine hangs a large slab of metal with a Vince Lombardi quote painted on it in slanted white cursive lettering:

*Winning is not a sometime thing, it's an all the time thing. You don't win once in a while, you don't do things right once in a while, you do them right all of the time. Winning is a habit. Unfortunately, so is losing. There is no room for second place. There is only one place, and that's first place.*

When it was too early or too late and there was nothing good on TV, I would play one of the *Rocky* movies on the DVD player as I commanded the machine to move faster and faster under my feet. My mom has always loved *Rocky*—"Yo, Adrian!"

my parents often say to each other—and though I didn't understand why, I wanted to. As I got deeper into my runs, I always hoped my dad would open the door and come down, like he sometimes did. "What's going on down here," he would always ask as he descended the steps. Then, lingering to catch the end of a fight scene, he'd say something like, "I don't know, Rock, I think you're going to get beat." Whenever my dad was witnessing the running body doing its work, I tried to move as smoothly and easily as possible—effortless and pristine. Whenever he eventually found whatever he came down looking for and climbed back up the stairs, I imagined one day reading an article in a magazine, or seeing my dad being interviewed on TV. I imagined a journalist asking, "What was Emily like as a young athlete?" And I imagined him recalling the scene: body floating and gliding over the smooth belt of the treadmill, early morning, watching Rocky Balboa chase chickens, smiling like she thinks she could have caught 'em, seeming whole and healthy, happy and hardworking.

Once I was back to school in late-January, my parents drove the hour south to take me out to lunch for my twentieth birthday. The day felt like the weather: bitter cold, low-hanging blanket of clouds. For lunch I chose the worker-owned co-op for Mexican food reimagined through the lens of white Appalachian hippies. My dad was frustrated when his burrito took a long time to come out. I was too preoccupied by the task of eating and the risk of eating to feel any sense of whatever I was supposed to feel. It was the day before my birthday, anyway. Olivia would be at the art studio all day, and as the conversation turned dull, I craved the emptiness our dorm room promised.

Later, when my dad pulled the car back into the parking lot of Boyd Hall and I reached for the door, my mom said, "One more thing," as she turned around, smiling. "She won't eat that," my dad said, as my mom showed me the homemade apple pie she had cooling under her seat. It was the most beautiful and wretched thing I'd seen all day. Apple pie was my favorite dessert before dessert became threatening. "She can share it with her friends," my mom said in protest. I smiled or tried to smile, the bottom of the glass pie dish warm in my hands.

Back in my room, I decided I wanted to get it over with—like a breakup or an exam or the first two-and-a-half miles of a 5K. I started by cutting out a reasonable triangle and drowning it in milk—the way I used to like it—then stuck the bowl in the microwave. As the seconds counted down, my sense of doom grew. All that sugar and fat and butter and carbs and calories and goo spinning around in the light like a grotesque ballet. My vision blurred and my mind moved to tomorrow's workout: First Street hill repeats. You have to keep up with Juli. Indoor meets are coming up—you need to get down to your racing weight. If you eat one bite, you'll eat the whole thing. You can't control yourself. You ate too much at lunch anyway. Too many chips, too much guacamole.

The beep of the microwave was startling. My fork was in the bowl before the bowl was all the way out of the microwave, but before I finished chewing the first bite, I started walking down the hallway, warm bowl in hand, toward the bathroom. I dumped it in the trash, banged the bowl against the can. Then, I walked back to the room, grabbed the rest of the pie, and headed back to the bathroom. After more dumping, scraping, banging, I sunk my hands into the bag, underneath the apple pie ruins, and pulled up a bunch of empty shampoo bottles, crumpled paper towels, and mascara-coated makeup wipes. I tried to arrange it all to cover the gooey and golden remains. I pulled out more paper towels and crumpled and layered them on top. I washed the dish with hand soap in the sink. I couldn't wait for the next morning, when the women who cleaned the building would take out the trash. I wanted that pie very far from me.

But the scent of pastry filled the hallway. It followed me back to my room; I locked the door. I laid down in bed and looked at the running watch on my wrist. My parents were probably still driving somewhere on State Route 33, or they were pulled off at a gas station, my mom might be walking the aisles, picking out candy. When they got home, the scent of the pie would be there. It would follow them like it followed me, into the kitchen and out into the living room, where my dad would take a deep breath and sigh and turn on the TV.

By spring, the darkness of the season before seemed to lift. Maybe it was my love for track; my drive to train for and race the 10K. Twenty-five grueling laps around and around the oval; 6.2 miles to cover with whatever strength and grit you could muster. Maybe it had something to do with being single and the sense of freedom that came with that. Between the end of my disappointing cross country season and the start of outdoor track, I walked over to The Vic and broke up with Aaron, having decided that he was holding me back. Maybe it was that my binge eating had been physically restorative, even if every time it happened I felt ravaged emotionally. Maybe it had something to do with the sky clearing up, the sun showing through.

On an early-May afternoon, a few weeks after I had run what I didn't know would be the race that turned to scar inside me, I had three more 1,000-meter repeats. I'd put two in the bank already. The caffeinated energy gel I'd squeezed into my mouth an hour before, on the way out to the track, had my body buzzing. Even inanimate objects looked warm and happy. I swung my hips loose and looked at Rick and said, "I'm ready."

He looked down at the stopwatch in his hand. "Ten more seconds." We were working methodically, trying to tune the running body to my goal pace for the Regional 10K. I'd even been doing most of my hard training in the heat of the day to prepare for early June in Jacksonville. It was the biggest race of my life, Rick said, and we were trying to do everything right.

Back then, when the running body had done its job, had

hardened under the work, ran the miles, repeated over and over the fluid motions of drills and core work and strength work, had gone to sleep early night after night, feeling tired legs buzz to their own state of rest, had felt them stride through dreams, imagined and fantasized and watched the race play out in my mind, so much so that the body felt it too, had heard the gun go off time and time again and felt the body lurch forward without thinking, settling into the pace, had felt the pace in the bones, knew it better than oneself, for the self had begun to fade, letting the running body take the space it needs, the self so willing, when all of that had been done, and more, of course there is more, so much more I'm now forgetting, on race mornings, the running body coated half a bagel with peanut butter and sliced a banana and sipped black coffee from a hotel mug, and the running body thought the hay is in the barn or the miles are in the bank and thought, hesitantly, and cautiously, as to not raise her heart rate before the race even began, that soon it will be time to go to the well or to put the hammer down or take the pain or simply to race. For that word, over so many miles and mornings and seconds ticking on stopwatches strapped around wrists, hiding sharp tan lines, that word did not lose meaning but only gained it. As the running body chipped away at the self as necessary, that word was given more and more meaning until its meaning surrounded all other meanings. I began to see the race inside and outside of all other things, by which I mean, the race became godly, and I grew wild with faith in its power to save me. On race mornings, the running body was so eager focused ready to get on its feet I could hardly speak.

I'd qualified for the NCAA Regional at a small meet in Hillsdale, Michigan. On that night, it seemed like Rick believed in what the running body was doing. Like he wasn't surprised to hear his voice calling out 81, 82, 83, 82.5 lap after lap. "Right there Pife. Right there. You're doing it. Just keep cruising. You're right there. Head up. Torso forward. Keep moving. Right there." His words mixed with the tiny molecules of moisture dancing underneath the stadium-light glow. During that race, one of the only few I can still feel, as if my cells carry its markings, Rick's voice anchored me inside my body until around mile three, when it all went dark. I was no longer there, as far as I can tell—I remember nothing but a sense of floating. I heard Rick's voice from under water so deep. But I don't mean to say I felt a sense of watching the running body race from sky. It wasn't only out-of-body, it was out-of-mind.

There's a Dick's Sporting Goods commercial that opens by saying, "There are trace amounts of gold in every human body." A montage of famous athlete bodies dripping sweat, grunting, pushing and pulling weight flashes across screen. "The highest concentration of gold is found in the heart. We are all made from this ancient and rare material. Gold. It's in us all. Only some have the strength to dig it out." The athletes are gritty, their bodies hard and working. Blood covers boxer Claressa Shields' face like war paint. It's a beautiful commercial, but when you know what I know, you know gold means nothing. Because if you dig very deeply into your body, you will find an incredible absence of your being. You will find nothing. You will, in fact, experience a kind of de-creation. It will be temporary—this pass into and through nothingness.

Before she starved to death, Simone Weil wrote, "Once we have understood that we are nothing, the object of all our efforts is to become nothing." For me too, the effort became irresistible. I could not resist.

For me pistols pointed toward the sky were like flashes of lightning. First the crack then the smoke. I no longer know what I felt. I only know that I felt it—a slipping away, a vanishing. After the gun went off and the smoke came, I'd feel pain then pain then pain then pain then, sometimes, I'd feel a crossing *over* something, or *into* something. I could no longer think. I think I disappeared is what I'm saying. No white light. No total darkness. Nothing to see. Not even the absence of presence. It was erasure—complete. All of me that was not the running body—the body running—left. To be gone was to be free. But it was only temporary.

People say you can do whatever you put your mind to. They say, "Mind over matter." But it always seemed as if my mind was in the way of my matter, sending out its frantic messages, trying to put a stop to my body and the pain it was making as it careened down the track. I noticed that, during my best races, it wasn't that my mind had conquered my body, it was that my body became engulfed deeply in the flames of its own pain, climbing up through the Achilles and calves and down from the heart and the lungs and meeting in the center and spreading through to each and every cell working to move move move. What I'm saying is I learned that I must welcome the pain inside, allow it to replace my thoughts and beliefs, my stories and identity. I had to stop feeling the pain so that I could become the pain, to put it simply.

After crossing the finish line in Hillsdale, the running body laid flat on a patch of earth, face tilted up to the moving sky. I suppose it was waiting. One, two, three—eventually, what was hollowed undergoes a process of refilling. Eventually, I started coming back inside my body.

After races like this, races where I left and let the body do its work without the rest of me interrupting, I couldn't sleep. It felt like I was waiting up, waiting for something, waiting for the rest of me to make it back from whatever trip I had taken, wherever I had gone. That night in Hillsdale, with a hotel room to myself, I turned on the TV. It was three in the morning, and the tallest guy from my high school showed up on the screen. B. J. was playing on one of the NBA's minor league teams, and his was one of the top plays in a show called something like "Biggest Sports Bloopers of the Week." I thought about B. J. (whether he was watching, how he might be feeling), and thinking about him seemed to complete the process of self returning to body. I never knew what to call it. It was always just an absence, or an empty, and then a presence—something like the feeling of arriving home after a long day. I turned off the TV. I woke up a few hours later desperately hungry.

But back there on the track that early-May day, weeks removed from this race in Hillsdale, with the sun and its shining, I was moving slightly too fast, a couple of seconds off pace, and Rick kept telling me to slow down and control my speed—to imagine having five miles to go, to imagine it all catching up to me. After the third repeat, when I proved that I could not slow down, could not control my speed, he changed the workout and said that, instead, I would do 200s until I hit the pace within less than half a second every single time. He told me to feel the pace and see the race: the runners on the line with me, the anguish excitement pain coming. Before each repeat I tried to settle my legs, lungs, and feet as if before the gun, smoke, elbows shoving. Working in this way felt more like programming than running, but with Juli studying abroad for the semester in France, I bathed in the warmth of Rick's undivided attention.

When I was finally able to put the running body on cruise control and began hitting the pace almost exactly, Rick and I grew relaxed and were smiling and laughing, talking about how hot humid exciting it will all be once we got down to Florida in a couple of weeks. We talked about how this was a big step for me—literally a step toward the national meet—and that I was ready. My limbs felt light. I could see my eyes—wild—reflecting back to me in the mirrored-lenses of Rick's aviators. I could see what he was seeing.

A tear came and I wiped it away quickly, shook out my arms and shoulders before one last repeat. Halfway around the oval one last time, hitting the pace perfectly. On my three-mile cooldown, I begged myself over and over: Never forget this feeling, never forget this feeling, never forget this feeling. But I've been forgetting.

I did not race well down in Jacksonville. I could not accept the pain, I suppose, could not vanish into the running. I felt like I had done something, though, just by making it there. Felt like I had nearly touched something that had seemed untouchable the year before. At our end-of-season awards banquet, I received MVP. On the plane ride home from Florida, I suggested to Rick that I increase my mileage over the summer. I said that I was feeling good and strong and that my body could handle it. I knew very few collegiate women were running over eighty miles a week, but this knowledge never deterred me. By the time the plane landed, Rick had agreed to my proposal. "Just be careful," he probably said, though I can't remember and would not have listened either way.

In June, my mom and sister and I spent a few days at Virginia Beach. It ended up being too windy and chilly to do anything but walk around in sweatshirts zipped up over our dry swimsuits. We didn't know what to do with ourselves at night, so we all went to bed at nine. Then, my mom and I would wake up early to take off on our separate runs. On the last day, it warmed up just enough for us to spend a few hours at the beach. Walking beside each other across the gray sand, my mom said I looked stronger this summer than last summer. I knew that by stronger she also meant bigger, but I didn't care as much as I would have months before. Mostly because I *felt* stronger, and also because running had been going well, and also because I knew I had the whole summer to whittle away again.

Slowly over the months before, my obsession with not eating anything had turned into an obsession with eating only "the right" things. I continued to eat very large amounts of food, often with the same out-of-control feeling that descended on me at my grandparents' house during Christmas, but my rigid rules around "good" and "bad" foods offered a sense of control, and because I felt more in control, I felt like I was doing much better than I was the summer before. Though I remained in the deep and the dark of the well, I had clawed my way closer to the surface. I could see the light. I wanted to let it warm me.

# II.

SOMETIMES THE BODY is tired, and sometimes the body is tired of being. The bones begin weakening. Muscle fibers stay torn for weeks. The face looks haunted then hollow then deserted entirely. Ankles tied together with a piece of cloth. Not supposed to ring hands when they fall asleep or clear the throat to scream. "What kind of music would you like?" Two 45-minute sessions of the machine whirring and clicking and taking images of the bones and their failings.

Needle in vein, needle in vein, needle in vein. Dark red blood filling. Always brought to the surface instantly; as if, all that time, it had been looking for an emergency exit out of the body. Results in ten days, two weeks, three. Results inconclusive.

All of this seemed like it happened quickly, but really, it had been happening for a long time, very slowly. That is, I suppose, the modus operandi of overuse injuries.

"I wish I would have done what you did," a friend from the cross country team said once as we searched for a parking spot at Nike

World Headquarters in Beaverton, Oregon. It was late winter in 2015, the cherry blossoms already blooming. I had just turned twenty-three, quit my job as an editorial assistant in New York City, gone back to Ohio to apply to graduate programs, then flown out to do some copywriting for his startup ad agency. We were late for a three o'clock meeting with brand marketing. I watched out the window as a group of professional Oregon Track Club runners moved easily over a wood-chip path on their way to the Michael Johnson Track, the 400-meter oval tucked inside a leafy green forest at the edge of Nike's campus. You don't know what I did, I kept thinking but not saying.

I told no one what I had gotten myself into, what I was, as they say, still going through. I would admit to nothing until I was farther away from the people and places that surrounded that summer and the cross country and track seasons that came after. And although I had been dangerously underfed, it seemed as if the running body that resulted in my undereating and overtraining had been encouraged, expected, and celebrated by nearly everyone surrounding me, especially our coaches. I received a plaque for "Most Improved Performer" after that summer. Juli received one for MVP. Then, because Juli was studying abroad during the spring track season, the MVP award was given to me. And even as I name what happened, what I did, how I tried to rewrite my story, so much of it still feels unspeakable to me. I still say, to certain friends and family, "I didn't know what I was doing. I didn't know how to eat enough to maintain a healthy weight while running eighty-five-mile weeks. I didn't feel it happening until it was too late." Like it wasn't intentional: the burning up of body.

But it *was* intentional. Wasn't it? If the furnace is hot enough everything burns, goes the saying. Translation: If you're running enough, every bite will become energy. That means your ribs might poke through your skin, your cheeks might hollow, and your veins might protrude out of your muscles like tiny mountain ranges. But when there is nothing left to burn—no more food or fat to mine for fuel—muscle will engulf into flames and, eventually, bones will begin breaking.

Even two years removed from collegiate running, I didn't know how to admit to myself or anyone else that, for a period of time, I could not allow myself to eat enough to keep my body from evaporating. I didn't know how to get help, or if I needed it, or if I wanted it, or if I should just keep doing what I was doing until something or someone stopped me. I didn't know there would or could be long-term consequences. Or did I? Sometimes it seems like I must not have been able to think past the next season. Sometimes it seems like I must not have been able to think at all, or at least not clearly. After reading an early draft of this text, a writing teacher kindly noted, "It's about a smart person doing a stupid thing."

In the middle of a long hike just outside of Laramie, Wyoming, a new friend said, "Tell me the Emily Pifer story." It was late summer, 2015, and I had just moved to town to start a graduate program in creative writing. I was having a hard time breathing, up over 8,000 feet, but in between gasps I told him my story would be boring. Then, for the first time, I began trying to tell him what I'm—right now, in this bleeding brief blurring instant—trying to tell you:

"Now my fractures are phantoms. There's pain where no pain exists."

"I started going to Mass again every Sunday—I prayed for nothing but fast racing."

"After the first fracture and just before the second, our trainer sent me to the sports psychologist and he asked me how I felt and for an hour I smiled, laughed, and expressed an uncomplicated love for the act of running. Kept telling him I was fine, fine, fine. And I actually fooled him! He even sent me an email after. He said he didn't think we needed to keep meeting."

I remember, after that last bit, invoking David Foster Wallace and *Infinite Jest*, which I had read in bars and coffee shops across every part of Portland in the months before, always dressed in flannel and denim, always stewing about something, like whether I would ever be a "real writer" or whether I would ever be able to "*really* run" again or who I would have to become instead.

I wanted so badly to tell a good clean story. On that hike, on these pages. But I don't have what the fiction writers have—that knack for narrative, for creation, for world-building. I suppose I have always been drawn to the messiness of happened and happening.

The way trying to make story out of memory is woven with failure, doubt, uncertainty. How the closer you think you are to knowing, seeing, understanding, the blurrier it all becomes. What's the ancient saying? I'm thinking of the one that goes: The more you know, the more you realize you don't know. Let us not forget, though, that many of our ancient men—the ancient Greeks so claimed by the West—had a great distrust for writing. They thought its power was too dangerous, too menacing.

I suppose I do as well. Can we control what we inherit, whether it be through the violence of culture or the violence of nature? Though my distrust is not so much for the practice of writing, but for the language I must use to do it (aren't all binary systems faulty?), and most of all, for myself. When Didion wrote, "We tell ourselves stories in order to live," let's not forget she meant myths. Perhaps this is why, when it comes to the ancient Greeks and Romans (both their men and their myths), I am most drawn to Gorgias and the sophists. Gorgias believed that language was everything—the *only* thing. He did not believe in absolute truths; he believed in situation and context. He believed in a whole world of maybes.

Here is why I am telling you this. In October of 2012, after my first fracture had healed, Juli and I were standing in the hallway between our second-floor bedrooms in the apartment we shared with Olivia and Melissa on a street called Foster Place, which rested diagonally across from The Vic. It must have been a day or two after we each had our appointments with the sports psychologist. Juli didn't know she was on the cusp of a very fast and promising indoor season (there would be articles, interviews, championships), I didn't know I was on the cusp of another fracturing.

"He thinks we should start meeting twice a week," Juli said, reading an email from the sports psychologist off her phone (if my memory, as they say, serves me). I then told her that he emailed me too. I told her he said he'd be happy to continue meeting, but that he didn't really think it was necessary.

After the hike in Laramie, my brain kept getting snagged on this particular part of the story. There were holes, it seemed. Did I read my email from the psychologist to Juli the way she read me hers, straight off her phone screen? And would a psychologist even email something like that to a potential patient? I couldn't see my part of the scene clearly, and eventually, the holes started to feel more like rips in the fabric of a constructed reality. Eventually, I logged onto my undergraduate email account, thankful it was never shut down, surprised to feel my username and password float through my fingers to the keys without thinking, and searched for the sports psychologist's name in my inbox—still etched in memory.

From: Emily Pifer
Sent: Monday, October 15, 2012 12:53 p.m.
To: Dr. ▉▉▉▉▉▉
Subject: RE: sports psychology referral

Dear Dr. ███████,

I wanted to thank you again for meeting with me yesterday. I really gained a lot of insight from our time together and know that I will benefit from our discussion. After reflecting about our meeting though, I do not think that regularly meeting with you is necessary for me. Although I really liked it, I know that I may benefit even more from continuing to think things through for myself. That being said, I hope to continue my connection with you and will not hesitate to seek your guidance out if there is a need in the future. Thank you again, I hope you have a wonderful fall.

Sincerely,
Emily

From: Dr. ███████
Sent: Tuesday, October 16, 2012 5:06 p.m.
To: Emily Pifer
Subject: RE: sports psychology referral

Dear Emily,

Thank you for your message. I completely understand. My door is always open if you would like to again.

I bid you a good performance all around!

Kind regards,
Dr. ███████

I lied to Juli in the hallway that night, then I lied until the lie turned true in my mind. By the time I told my friend during our hike that I fooled the sports psychologist, I didn't even know I was lying. I suppose, then, you can consider this a warning. This isn't what happened, it's what I remember happening.

Doesn't it seem haphazard, anyway? The way things do or do not become part of our stories? Which is perhaps also to say, the way things do or do not become part of our bodies? Doesn't it seem like nothing just happens? Doesn't it seem like everything that will ever happen has already been happening for a very long time, very slowly? The past and present and future seem to bleed together desperately and without asking. Is that why I cannot keep from looking behind me? This is of course not a question but a begging; I cannot stop looking.

BEFORE MY GRANDMA JANE and Grandpa Denny and their four children then teenagers lived in the house deep in the Appalachian mountains, up in Tucker County, at the bottom of Location Road, Jecky Adams lived there. She died there too. There was a small house fire. She got caught in the flames. Her body burned, but some part of her stayed. In that old house, Jecky Adams's ghost performed little hauntings.

"Weren't you sick?" I asked my grandma once, after she finished the briefest version I'd ever heard of a Jecky Adams story I'd heard many times before. She stiffened and said she wasn't sick.

"I thought that's why the house was a mess? I thought that's why you were resting on the couch?" I asked.

"No," she said in that stern, worn way of a woman worn stern.

But between you and me, Jecky Adams had a thing for domestic upkeep. She only showed up for her little hauntings when the house got out of order, and sometimes when my grandma tells it, she says she'd been sick for days, and she was lying on the couch, facing the wall, trying to get some rest, ignoring the accumulation of a few days' mess.

And that's when she felt touched. "By who?" She felt it on her shoulder. Gentle, then gone. She called out to my grandpa— "Denny?"—but he was across the street working.

"It was Jecky?" I always ask. And my grandma always nods her head, a smile spreading from her eyes.

I'm not sure when Jecky Adams lived in that old house, or when her life burned out. Maybe it's not even the truth about

Jecky that most interests me. Maybe it's the way the stories about her hauntings move from telling to telling, body to body. And how in this way, the happened bleeds into the happening. How once haunted is always haunting.

In 1985 it started raining in Tucker County and didn't stop for a long time. The rain kept coming and coming. That's how Jecky Adams died a second time. One hundred homes were destroyed in the flood. Many of them up and floated away (my uncle and aunt's house did). And while that old house hung on to its place in the ground, Jecky's ghost drowned.

What I mean is this. After the flood, Jecky never showed up again. Like all that time there were parts of her still burning. Like all that water finally extinguished the flames. Like every little haunting was a cry for help: Put me out.

"What did Jecky look like?" I asked once.

"Oh." My grandma looked at me hard. "She was just a regular woman."

She said those words as if they explained everything.

That old house is starting to fall down now, but you can still go inside, and you can still reach up and trace your finger along the water line.

In *Ways of Seeing*, John Berger writes how the sight of fire must mean something different now than it did when men believed in the physical existence of hell. How they must have been haunted by what remains after the flames. How there was both a pain in the burn and a pain in the ashes.

Fire teaches us that where there is destruction, there is debris. A scientist friend once told me that some species of plants must, every season, burn down in flames to grow up again. And that some animals can only live in places that have burned recently. These beings make their homes out of ruin; their lives out of burning.

When I think of these beings, I think of a news story from the summer of 2016. I must have been back in Ohio, visiting my parents, when the local stations started reporting about the teenage girl from Cincinnati who traveled to Jackson, Wyoming, with an organization called Groundwork USA. On her last day helping to restore a system of trails in Grand Teton National Park, she told a group of her friends that she was going to the bathroom, said she would be back soon. Two days and hundreds of bodies searching for her body later, she was found less than four miles from where she was last seen working. Except she'd cut and dyed her hair. She'd changed her clothes. And when the rescuers called her name, she ran the other way. The girl's name is Fauna but that only matters because it's a beautiful name, one from which I cannot imagine running. "I know this is not something she would do of her own accord," her math teacher said in an interview with the local news. Apparently, people started thinking someone forced the changes on her. There were theories. Why would someone want to mask her identity? Kidnapping, maybe. She couldn't have done this to herself. Why would she? She was so grounded, so happy. Flourishing, really.

After the investigation into her temporary disappearance and reconstruction of identity returned nothing, her family started denying that she had changed anything at all and ignored her given name when called. And the news stories reported that she's doing fine now, and has returned home, back to her "old self," to the relief of all.

"Who will foot the bill for her large search party?" The articles asked near their ends, and according to them, it was still a matter to be determined.

Around this same time, my mom and I, scrolling through channels, came across a documentary about "Baby Jessica." As the story goes, in October 1987, Baby Jessica, who was eighteen months old, fell into an abandoned water well just outside the fence in her aunt's backyard in Midland, Texas. She got trapped deep down under the well's shaft. According to the documentary, the whole country watched, everyone holding their breath, while they prayed for the baby's safety. Two and a half days later, she was rescued: dirty and damaged and crying, but okay. Now, the woman Baby Jessica became says she doesn't remember any of it happening. Her scars, which were covered by bangs, remain as evidence of injury, carriers of story.

I have read on the internet that any loss can lead to grieving. Loss of a dream. Loss of safety. Loss of what you cannot name, or at least, cannot speak. Loss of a feeling. A feeling deep in your body. A feeling of belonging in your body. Loss of a belief. A belief that your body is an entity separate from your mind, and therefore can be controlled under its jurisdiction. A loss of control. Loss of hope, faith, ritual, routine. Loss of love, even if the love was not made of the stuff of love, but became love. There is no such thing as a normal loss, the internet tells me, or a normal response to it. And like how every instance of trauma is unique, every response to loss, trauma, wounding is personal and situational. Under this framework, every injury is an invention. Every wound is its own world. And the process of grieving is not, as we would like to believe, linear. It is not, as psychiatrist Elisabeth Kübler-Ross had us thinking in 1969 with the publication of her groundbreaking *On Death and Dying*, a universalized, forward-moving, and steady-paced march from loss to denial, then on through anger, depression, and bargaining until we finally reach acceptance, that distant and oh-so-promising psychological mountain peak. Rather, as Kübler-Ross argues now, it is a cycle—made from not one circle, but many, concentric and overlapping, sticky and slippery.

Still, while I can get down with believing any loss can lead to grieving, there must be levels to loss, levels to grief. I try often to remember: You have lost so little. You have only lost yourself. No, not even that. You have only lost who you thought yourself to be. "We become ourselves," Patti Smith wrote. I both love and feel resistance to this sentiment, but it doesn't matter how I feel, I have no evidence to the contrary.

Freud had much to say about grief too. According to him, the sustaining of a lost object—the psychic figure that emerges from an ungrieved or unacknowledged loss—leads to heightened identification, self-beratement, and feelings of unresolved anger and love toward the lost object or Other. This is, according to Freud, the recipe for melancholia. In this way, to be melancholic is to inhabit the purgatory between loss and grieved.

But it's not that I have not grieved—*I have grieved*—it's that I have not reached the end of my grieving. I have denied and been angry, I have fallen inside depression and I have clawed out by the teeth of three hundred bargains, and I have accepted what I did to my body and I have accepted the consequences, only to eventually slip again, back into the loss.

What happened? You are asking. Be more clear, you are saying. But I have been wanting to show you what looking at this wound looks like to me.

SOMETIMES, OVER THE phone usually, Juli and I talk about that summer—that summer when we became consumed by running, that summer when we became running bodies—and the cross country and track seasons that came after like it was all a bad dream. Sometimes we talk about it like, even if it was, all we want to do is fall back asleep. In our inflection we negotiate the tensions dwelling in our distant bodies, between what happened and what's happening. Sometimes we're trying to find what's lost. Sometimes we're just circling the drain.

"It's a year I'm always trying to get back to. And recreate. And I can't—I've been failing for years. I want it so bad that you'd think it would come easy. I can recite everything I did in my day, and I know you probably can too. It's not like this mystery. But there's this resistance to it because I know how difficult it was and I know how much of a non-person I was, and I guess I've just been experimenting with the question: Can I have the same success but remain a whole person? And so far that answer is no."

After that summer she became an All-American four times over; my bones began fracturing. What we talk about when we talk about running are moments of surface scarring. Quiet trauma that gets stuck inside the revolving doors of our memories. Unable to move deep inside where the ways they mark us can take on new meanings.

"I can't remember if it was my junior or senior year—it probably happened during both, but it was in the wintertime. I went to the gym to do core work, and I was in a room surrounded by all of these mirrors, and I was so disgusted with what I saw. I just sat and cried and then left."

When she said this, I began calculating. This—the mirror, the crying, the sudden horror of facing her body—happened either less than a month after she earned her first All-American title in cross country or less than a month after she earned her second.

"I remember standing on the starting line at Nationals and looking over at another runner, then looking down at me. I was finding all of the things that were better about her body. And I was the fittest I'd ever been in my life."

When Juli said this, I could feel her staring up at the ceiling of her and Chris's new house in Eugene. Chris was our assistant coach for a year before he left Ohio and moved out to Oregon to pursue running professionally. Chris and Juli slowly began talking more after they spent several days together in Europe during the London Olympics in 2012. Chris had traveled over to spectate; Juli was just wrapping up her time studying abroad in France. Once she returned to Athens and he to Eugene, they would FaceTime for hours the way that distant lovers do. He would fly back to Ohio to watch her race, then stay in our apartment on Foster Place. Though that is their story and not mine, I can't help but imagine their lives together now. I can't help but imagine a whole life built on their hardened running bodies, which promise nothing more than to eventually go weak, over the time and distance, that none of us, in the end, are able to overcome. I imagine cabinets filled with four different nut butters, bananas ripening for muffins because on

Sunday there will be company, and locally-sourced energy: bars, bites, balls, nibs, jelly.

"Why don't I ever think about the first time I won Regionals in cross country, you know? Or the first time I won Conference?"

There were over one thousand miles between Juli and I, she in Eugene and me in Laramie, and in that distance, we lost something. But still, I know I didn't need to tell her that for me, too, it was the injury at the forefront of my memory. It was the pain inflicted. Crimes against body. I tell her anyway. I tell her about the day before and how I'd taken a bite of a chocolate peanut butter PowerBar and how it tasted like starving. Like the middle of the day in the middle of seventy- or eighty-mile weeks and the first days of fall semester after that summer when I was trying my best to stick to my summer routine of only eating enough to say yes if anyone asked if I was eating. Suddenly, I felt an urge to ask Juli if she had been eating.

"Earlier this week I was thinking about a time that summer when I went to my friend's pool party and borrowed my sister's bathing suit and it fit perfectly, or even was a little too big. And it was the first time where I felt like my body was going in the right direction. I remember thinking: It's working. But then, I was still really concerned with how all the boys saw me and if they thought I was too fat or whatever."

Hanging over the rest of our conversation was a nostalgia gone stale. The worry I so often feel for her is, of course, worry, too, for myself. If she's still so fucked up, where does that leave me?

The way we say goodbye is often guarded and relieved—at least it feels that way. Because to face Juli is to face me. And what we did to our bodies—together and separately. And how, even now, we're making circles around the same things.

When I spread anything—butter, avocado, jelly—the intimation shoots my mind back in time to Juli and me making peanut butter sandwiches for lunch. Around 7:30 each morning, in the dining hall, right after our morning runs or morning swims or morning sessions in the weight room, feeling weak as we squatted and pushed and pulled weights that looked cartoonish compared to what the swimmers and wrestlers and football players were lifting; right after two eggs over easy and blessedly calorie-free coffee.

Then it's September, October, November. I've been in such an extreme caloric deficit for so many months, I can no longer go the whole day without eating, but in a sandwich, at least, I can easily control how much I allow my body, the calories and fat and carbohydrates I'm in-taking. A sandwich isn't like a bowl of cereal (so easily replenished) or even a salad (where the options for adding on are endless). A sandwich, compared to the many other options, is way less threatening. In between two slices of wheat bread, we cannot allow ourselves to get too greedy.

I wait as long as I possibly can. I wait for eight o'clock then nine o'clock then ten—finally, comes the mercy of eleven. I eat the sandwich in Poli Sci or Sociology or wherever. Once it's gone, I place the bag under my desk, leaving it open in my lap. I lick the tips of my fingers then, reaching my hand in, gather the tiniest bits of nourishment and place them on my tongue, one by one.

When I was just beginning to try and face what I did to my body, I read a blog post by a runner from Iowa State trying to do and face similar things. She says she wouldn't even eat peanut butter sandwiches during her most dangerous phase of undereating and overtraining. She says they made her feel too out of control and too heavy and too guilty. I spent the rest of the afternoon thinking: I wasn't even good at starving.

I've looked at the medical records—

> HISTORY: Patient is an avid runner, has had pain in the forefoot for 2-½ weeks. Evaluate for stress fracture.

—tracing what happened—

> FINDINGS: Intense marrow edema is noted involving the base of the 3rd metatarsal with extension of edema throughout the remainder of the ray except for sparing of the distal neck and head.

—with the only real and hard and objective evidence I have.

> Subtle transversely oriented hyperintensity compatible with nondisplaced fracture (stress fracture).

Sometimes, I feel the words there like boiling water threatening the edges of its pot—

> CONCLUSION: 1. Nondisplaced stress fracture at the base

*of the 3rd ray without evidence for extension into the tar-
sometatarsal joint.*

—but I was never diagnosed with anything

*2. Capsulitis above the metatarsophalangeal joint of the
great toe with valgus orientation of the distal phalanx of
the great toe.*

—other than a series of fracturing.

*3. May see additional findings above. Thank you for the
opportunity to provide your interpretation.*

No one labeled me with any particular disorders or urged me to
seek treatment.

*History: Athlete complained of pain during the summer
break.*

There were just a handful of days lost—

*She saw an ortho physician at home.*

—to electromagnetic radiation and needles through veins and
questions re: scales of pain.

*MRI shows a stress fx.*

It's all so concise and clean.

*Boot for 2 ½ weeks all of the time.*

Fractured.

*No pain when walking now.*

Fractured.

*Has been swimming, water running and biking without
boot.*

Fractured.

*Please follow up.*
The records report no sign of non-physical injury.

> *Findings: MRI-Stress fx. Diagnosis: Stress fx of left 3rd metatarsal.*

Before I emailed the head of the athletic training department for the records—

> *Treatment: Boot for 3+ more weeks. Follow-up with X-Ray. OK to swim. Boot at all other times.*

—I texted Katie, who was our athletic trainer during my time on the team.

> *Recommendations: No practice until _____.*

"Do you know how I can get my hands on my medical records?" I asked.

> *History: Ath. is having pain in inguinal area.*

"Why do you want them?" She texted back.

> *P+ c arom/rrom of iliopsoas. P+ tolerable while running 8/10 P+ post-activity.*

Juli happened to call just ten minutes after I'd opened the fat envelope of medical language and disks I didn't have a drive for.

> *Developed a limp while walking.*

I'd already spread every page around me—

> *History: Pain has not decreased c 5 days of steroids and 4 days of rest.*

—like I was the sun—

> *Imaging?*

—and they were planets revolving.

*Pain on pubic bone when walking/running and standing on left leg.*

I had already read a few—

*Indication: Left pubic rami pain that shoots into the left knee.*

—felt sideswiped—

*Pain for 4 weeks.*

—gave in to crying.

*Patient is a distance runner and runs 8-12 miles per day.*

I said it seemed so clear—

*Findings: There's a marked marrow edema throughout the superior pubic ramus extending into the anterior and medial acetabulum on the left.*

—looking over the history of my body—

*There is an associated linear area of low STIR signal along the far lateral aspect of the suprapubic ramus on the left consistent with a nondisplaced fracture.*

—that I needed a kind of help I wasn't getting.

*There is also a marrow edema in the inferior pubic ramus with a nondisplaced fracture of anteromedial aspect of the inferior pubic ramus on the left.*

And that of all the information the records showed—

*There is edema in the soft tissue adjacent to the inferior pubic ramus and pubic symphysis on the left with marrow edema extending to the Parasymphyseal region on the left.*

—what they made most evident—

*There is a small synovial herniation along the lateral femoral head neck junction on the left.*

—was all that was missing.

*The hamstring tendon origin for the ischial tuberosity is intact bilaterally with subtle intermediate signal of the hamstring tendon origin on the left and mild adjacent soft tissue edema suggesting mild tendinitis.*

"Would sophomore or even junior year Emily," Juli started—

*There is mild increased STIR signal adjacent to the greater trochanter bilaterally suspicious for minimal bilateral trochanteric bursitis.*

—then stopped—

*A small amount of free pelvic fluid is likely physiologic.*

—a linguist, choosing her words carefully—

*Procedure: X-RAY EXAM OF PELVIS.*

—then kept going—

*Comparison: Pelvis MRI dated 15 February 2013.*

—"would she have wanted the help?"

*Findings: A fracture line is visible extending through the inferior pubic ramus inferiorly.*

"I don't know."

*The fracture involving the lateral aspect of the left superior pubic ramus is not visible although there is periosteal and cortical thickening that may reflect healing fracture.*

"Maybe."

After the first fracture healed, once I was cleared to run and began rejoining my team for practice, I could tell all the hours I had spent cross-training kept my heart and lungs conditioned and ready to work past burning. And I could tell the restrictive diet I had held myself to helped to maintain a semblance of the running body. But as soon as I hit the ground without my walking boot, I could tell something had changed. Something the doctor and trainers and my coaches couldn't see when they looked at me. All those weeks walking around campus in the boot seemed to knock my muscles and bones out of balance. But because I still looked "fit," and because my coaches knew how much work I had put in at the pool and in the water treadmill and on the bike and in the weight room, they looked at me and saw the opportunity for a few points at the conference meet. They were optimistic; I was trying to be. But I didn't know how to listen to my body, and even if I did, I would never have spoken up for it. I didn't demand, or even ask, that I use the medical redshirt available to me for the very situation I was in. Instead, after only a few weeks out of the boot, and already over halfway through the season, I began racing. Every step felt slow and heavy. I was simply not ready. Rather than working my way back up into a scoring position for my team (top five), I wasted my eligibility away in the back of the three races I ran that season.

It was my first time being so close to the last runner I could hear pity in the voices of anyone left on the sidelines cheering. Every step I took at the conference championship in Buffalo—a race I placed seventh in the year before—crushed my sense of identity, which was entirely bound up in not only my sense of myself as a runner, but my sense of myself as a fast, strong, and hard one. The second fracture that would come a few months later—just as I was beginning to feel at home in the running again, just as I was beginning to believe in the possibility of a return to running body—would make that race, in hindsight, seem like foreshadowing.

More than a month later, likely still licking my ego-wounds, Chris, who had been at the conference championship in Buffalo to watch Juli, emailed me from Eugene. "The Emily Pifer I saw run in Buffalo was not anything resembling the Emily Pifer from a year ago—and to be honest, it had little to do with your physical abilities," he wrote. These differences were not revealed in my legs or my lungs or even my heart, but in my eyes. "Those eyes," he wrote, "told a story of frustration and defeat." But he did not blame me; he understood the difficulty of injury. Even so, it was time, he said, "to turn over a new leaf." To leave the past in the past, "to rediscover that spark," to believe in my training. "You were a Regional qualifier in the 10K last year because you worked your ass off," he reminded me, and said I must stop asking questions and stop overthinking and get back to running hard and doing "all the little things."

I needed to quit giving myself outs and excuses because, after all, I was "still Ohio's 2nd best runner, an All-MAC performer, and a freaking Regional qualifier." I just needed to, "Think like it. Act like it. Train like it. Race like it. Do it." Chris reminded me that

I had six weeks to get myself back to racing shape, to break my personal records in the 3K and 5K. Then, he wrote, "The greatest detractor from high performance is fear," but if I could "eliminate that fear—not through arrogance or just wishing difficulties away, but through hard work and preparation," then I would be able to put myself "in an incredibly powerful position" to overcome my challenges. He left off by reassuring me that his message was "meant to be a good kick in the butt. Nothing more, nothing less."

Less than an hour later, I wrote Chris back thanking him for his note and promising him there were some fast races coming.

A month later I would be crawling around an indoor track and field complex in Bowling Green after racing a 3K. I would be crying and gritting my teeth. I would be trying to get away from all the other athletes and trainers and coaches. I would be all animal, looking for a lonely place to suffer. In the way that knowing is feeling and feeling is knowing, I would know and feel the way the whole jig was up. There was a fracture cutting right up the center of me and it would take over a year to heal, and by that time, I would have packed up my car and left Athens, then packed up my dad's truck and moved to New York City.

DURING MY SENIOR year, with my pubic ramus still fractured, I started applying for internships in New York. It seemed that Rick had written me off. I began to dread going to the athletic facilities, and I no longer felt a sense of belonging on my team. I would do just about anything to leave.

It was around this time when Melissa and I noticed that Juli, still one of the best runners in the country, had mostly stopped eating again. There was no sign of breakfast. "I read somewhere that you shouldn't eat until you feel hungry," she announced once on her way up the stairs after Melissa said something like, "No breakfast?" one morning. After her five- or six-mile morning runs, she always fixed a big jar of black tea. Sometimes, she would forget to take it upstairs with her, and she would climb down the steps as softly as she could, grabbing it off the counter and carrying it back upstairs as carefully, quickly, quietly as possible. She would always shut her door.

For lunch, she'd pop a bag of plain popcorn and take it to class with her in a Tupperware container. I felt angry all the time and sometimes, the energy of my anger felt like it was pointing toward Juli; she was still playing the game I had lost. Plus, with the pelvic fracture, I was not supposed to do any kind of exercise—no pool or bike or water treadmill. I was to remain as stationary as possible, and without a constant influx of post-workout endorphins flowing through my system, it turned out I was ill-equipped to soothe and care for my mental and emotional well-being.

There were whole days and evenings, though, when her

longing for invisibility and my sense of darkness would lift and we would spend time together and it would feel good and it would feel familiar. She would pour us both a glass of red wine and make large, beautiful meals in the kitchen—roasted vegetables and meat, cooked in butter like she had learned in France. Then, once Olivia and Melissa returned home, we would push the furniture to the side and spend hours dancing.

One evening, when she was out reading on the small balcony outside her bedroom, I must have limped out there and we must have got to talking. What I remember is the way she held me as I rocked and sobbed in her small arms. Eventually, I left town without saying anything to her about the frustration, envy, and worry I felt toward her and what she was doing. I did not say I could feel her fading away. And that what we once had felt like it was always slipping, sometimes slowly and sometimes quickly, through my fingers. And how that made me question everything. What kind of friendship had we constructed? Had it been built on a mutual longing for self-destruction, or at least, self-discipline gone dark? I probably didn't even ask how she was really doing. I probably thought I already knew.

At the end of fall semester, on an overcast Sunday, I packed my car quickly and left quietly. When Melissa, Olivia, and Juli returned from holiday break, they transformed my empty room into a space for yoga, core work, and stretching. When Melissa and Olivia threw parties, they would move out the yoga mats and people would play beer pong where my bed used to be. I liked knowing the place I occupied so often with misery, especially that last year, had turned into something fun and useful. Because my absence had been useful, it made me feel useful too.

On the twenty-first floor of the Hearst Tower where I was one of the new editorial interns for *Esquire* magazine, I felt the consequences of my leaving and sensed a new understanding dangling out ahead of me, in my line of vision, but still out of physical reach. I began asking the sorts of questions that would lead me here. Simple inquiries: What did I do to my body and why did I do it? Why did it feel like a necessity? And when I ate less and less and ran more and more, was it because of my love for running or something darker and more twisty? Was I ever really in control of anything?

While I spent long gray Saturdays walking from where I was renting a room in Hell's Kitchen down through Chelsea then over and through the East Village, I did not dream the dreams I planned to dream. I had already given them up. After just minutes in New York, I knew I was not going to be Joan or Patti. Instead, I dreamed old dreams. I longed for fiery lungs, legs, whole body burning. The past pulled me back—nostalgia, regret, remorse—as I tried to move forward. Which is what it always does, but I was too young and lucky and privileged to know it. By the time I got to New York in January it had been months since I had gotten the results that proved what my body already knew. My pelvic bone was still split in two, or had split again, I was never sure. I hated the answers so much I stopped asking questions. I had spent the half a year before that X-ray trying, off and on, to run on and through a broken body. At night I would close my eyes, trying to sleep, and see my bones shift like tectonic plates. I would see my blood swallowing them up in violent waves. I would watch my skeleton wash up in the tiniest pieces, more broken than before, like seashells on a shore.

In my second month in New York, I met Laurel, an NYU film student from Oregon and my first real friend in the city. I was eating dinner alone and she came right up to me as if I had been waiting for her. She took me to bars and parties and the good vintage stores. Even though she didn't really smoke, she always carried cigarettes—the orange pack of American Spirits—just in case. I never had to ask, "In case what?" I understood implicitly. Laurel ran recreationally and had trained and ran a half marathon the year before we met, back when she was still in Portland. I told her about my injuries, and admitted I really missed running and was hoping to build my mileage back up, to be and feel like a runner again. I told her a quarter of the story, the quarter of the story I had so far told myself.

Soon after meeting, Laurel and I began getting together for three- and four-mile runs a few times a week. It was the dead of winter: windy, gray, freezing. And moving forward felt awkward and forced, my body even more off-balance than it was after my first fracture, but chatting with Laurel about writing and filmmaking and what it might mean to try to make our lives as artists distracted me from spiraling, and after we finished, I often felt the buzz of hope coursing through me. Perhaps it was not hope exactly, perhaps it was just this: maybe maybe maybe. Around this time, I emailed Rick about returning to school to finish out my eligibility. I could pick up a master's degree, I suggested. I told him that I had been running consistently again, and that my bone felt healed. I told him that I may need some time to get back to where I was, but I believed I could. I don't know if I really believed any of these things, but even if they were pure fantasy, the thought of training hard, racing, and turning myself to running body again got me through long days of transcribing celebrity interviews and researching answers to readers' questions for the sex column. Rick never responded to that email though, and I haven't communicated with him since.

A few months later the freezing gray melted into spring. Melissa and Olivia and Juli graduated and I heard from each of them separately about how frustrating it was to get the apartment empty and clean and how strange it was to close the door and leave. Melissa would soon be off to Seattle for an internship with a startup sports drink company, Olivia would go back to Cleveland to work as a graphic designer, and Juli would move to Eugene to live with Chris and keep running competitively. Meanwhile, my internship was ending and even though I found the city too gray and too concrete, and I was not patient enough to find out what success might mean in the magazine industry, I figured returning to Ohio would be just another failure, so I moved from Manhattan to Brooklyn and got an editorial assistant job at another publication across town.

When my editor at *Women's Health* called me into her office to tell me I couldn't write about my injuries—or I could, but not in the way I had—I knew what she meant before she added, "I mean, we publish stories about women who suffer from insane diseases and lose limbs and stuff." I looked down at my feet. I said I understood completely, and I did. I knew there were much worse things. The article ran as "7 Ways to Mentally Heal from Your Injuries." It was positive, forward-looking, peppy.

But I wanted to write about how runners get hurt then heal then run more then get hurt again then heal again and on and on like that. I wanted to know what keeps people going back for more, and I wanted to know why, for me, and for many others, I presumed, the cycle seemed to break off somewhere between hurt and healed. I wanted to know why some days it felt like I had clawed myself out of a state of fracturing. And some days it felt different. Like I was sinking, over again, into the same bone-split. Like the fault line was etched somewhere deep, deeper than bone-deep.

But I have always understood the correct response to any weakening is strengthening. Tearing down to rebuilding. Breaking to healing. The correct response is to find meaning in the injury. To tell the story this way: I overcame. To say I hurt my body, but because it is a body, it healed. And because my body healed, I too have healed. And when I look back, I see a broken body but one that has taught me all the things that breaking is supposed to teach you. And look how I've let go, moved on, gotten over it. Look how I've told myself the story of a body redeemed. Look how I've organized my life around this new body, this new me. Look how much stronger and smarter and better I am. Look how I leave out the details that trouble me: all that I have not been able to pull myself out from, the phantom fractures and the way they haunt me, the dream that even on my least delusional days still pulses in my blood to the rhythm of maybe maybe maybe.

As a child, at home and school, I learned to associate war with dignity. I learned to associate warriors with strength, worthiness, utility. I understood that sacrificing the body for land and money and property was an expression of masculinity, and that masculinity was power.

I learned that masculine bodies were considered tougher and stronger and worth more than feminine bodies because masculine bodies were considered better at conquering. And so, quite early, I knew that as a girl it would be my duty to prove the worth and utility of my body to all the boys and men around me. And simultaneously, to look pretty.

In the post-9/11 of my youth, I learned that "going to war" was a highly respectable thing to do with the body. That battling, fighting, destroying were valuable trades. And that the damages and the scars were signs of triumph over something, which was the most important thing—the climax. I also understood that suffering toward the climactic triumph was commendable, but that once the climax was reached, the suffering should be regarded as over and the smaller losses put out of memory.

Rick would often say, "It's better to lose the battle but live to fight another day." When he said this, he was talking about taking care of small injuries before they became big injuries. But the meaning is always the same: If you live to fight another day, you might be able to win. And if you win, you can end the story, move on, get out clean. If you win, they can say, "He survived, didn't he?"

More recently, I learned that in ancient Greece, athletic training and competition was, at least partly, military training. It was not veiled as pastime, hobby, recreation, or entertainment. It was about more than fitness, or more accurately, it was precisely about fitness, but fitness was only the means. I learned that athletic training and competitions were regarded in esteem by those of both upper and lower classes, and that athletic training and education was, for "citizen class" boys and men, understood as two sides of the same coin, rather than opposing pursuits. I learned that Plato wanted to ban poetry from the polis, but I have never come across anything about him wanting to ban athletics.

Even though fitness was primarily approached as military training, I can't help but to imagine that many of the ancient Greek athletes thought or at least felt their military preparedness as secondary. There is great pain and pleasure and pain-as-pleasure in giving oneself over to the process of training, to the thrill of competing. I can't help but imagine our reasons for engaging in and becoming invested in sport have long been complicated and even contradictory.

Once I signed the contract to run at Ohio University, I adopted a sense that my body was no longer my property. Hunched over the coffee table in the living room, pen in hand, I remember a freedom washing over me. I felt released as I gave every inch of me over to my school, coaches, and team. I would be a small part of a whole history. In the years since that summer, I have felt a shameful pride for the line of fire in which I placed my body. Stood willing, ready.

Now I know I must either find an alternative way out of this story, or stay in here forever, spinning. I don't know if it's wrong or right to presume I have the ability (the power? the agency?) to make the choice. Of course the choice is yours to make, part of me says. If the choice were mine to make, why have I not made it? Another, or perhaps the same part, answers.

# III.

WHEN THE RUNNING BODY fractured from the center—right down the pubic bone—I felt a glimmering clarity. I knew I should not have done what I did to my body.

"I'm sorry," our team doctor said, his hands already moving toward me, "but I need to get my hands on it." Looking over at our athletic trainer, he said, "Katie, can you close that door?" Once the door was closed, he began using his hands to search my groin for the precise point of pain. My eyes flooded the instant he found it. I gritted my teeth to keep from screaming. Soon after, I was relieved when the scans proved my pain was not imaginary.

Now, I wish I could reach in and feel the once-fractured bones. I'd like to see, for sure, that there is no longer room for me to dwell inside the wounds, wounding. I have a theory that if I could just touch the evidence of their healing, something might emerge and that something might be a whole new way of being.

There is something sure about the site of injury. How it becomes a sight. How you can see the thing that happened and know, somewhere, inside your body, it had for a long time been happening. Especially when there are so many ways of wounding and getting wounded that involve no site and no sight—no way of seeing what happened or what is happening. Like losing bits of who you are or who you thought yourself to be. That sort of loss cannot be seen by machine. That sort of lostness goes undetected no matter the tests, ways of testing. And so how can you trust there is anything real about what you are feeling? I miss the sureness of hard, shiny disks delivered from the doctor's office and stress fractures shining on computer screens and heads nodding in knowing, seeing, believing the injury, and as it follows, believing me.

When a bone fractures, what happens in the split? I always imagined it there like a fixed emptiness. But now I wonder: Do fractures fold in on themselves? Does each side of split bone begin working to fill the empty at the moment of its conception? Is there any space at all? In MRI scans, fractures look like nothing more than scratches on hand-me-down coffee tables, and on X-ray readings, you often can't even see them. You can only see evidence of healing: scar tissue making its home. While waiting for results, between feeling and seeing the proof of my injuries, I would press hard through my skin along each millimeter of bone, grinding my teeth against the rush of tears when I found the precise spot of the fault line. The sting would ring through the rest of my body, and that's how I'd know. Every time the doctors would call with the news—three times in one year, starting one year after that summer—I had already believed in the presence of the fractures like someone who knows they have seen a ghost.

My mother's mother, my Grandma Sue, let my sister and I dress up in her lingerie. She called them her foo-foos. Sheer shorts with polka-dots and lace trimming. Silk camisoles loose on our torsos. She'd let us wash our hair with her expensive shampoo, then comb it straight back, each tooth moving across scalp, thick white towels across our shoulders to keep the backs of our nightgowns from dampening. Then we'd go to the kitchen, where she'd teach us ballet. Long past our usual bedtime, our right hands holding tight to the handle of her oven, left arms floating in the air, up for second position, then back down.

One afternoon Grandma Sue and I sat down on the floor in her living room. She handed me a pair of scissors and together we went through boxes of photographs, cutting out the faces and bodies of her ex-boyfriend, Buzz.

Even then, though I couldn't have been older than five or six, I think I understood the theory we were testing. Whether seeing the absence of the holes could be better than facing the presence of the images that once filled them. Because maybe on trash day, when all those little scraps of Buzz would be sent away, our memories would be fooled silly. And maybe if we just looked hard enough for long enough, the holes could signify the presence of something, rather than just the absence of another body.

Two days before Sue died of lung cancer—she started smoking when she was a teen—fire then smoke took over New York City. I only saw it on TV. Only remember the smoke filling the screen, then a change in scene: women running down the sidewalk with their high heels in their hands, their feet bare and slapping against concrete. I still think of those women and their panic every time I see a pencil skirt.

I was nine at the time and believed that everything that had happened and was happening and was ever going to happen must be connected. That together, it all must add up to something. I believed maybe, somehow, the same smoke that filled my grandma's lungs filled those hysteric New York City streets. I feel traces of those beliefs somewhere stilled in my body.

But the truth of the thing is that I remember the day my grandmother died because I got called out of school early. I spent the rest of that afternoon walking around and around the perimeter of the kidney bean-shaped pool, shifting between trying and not trying to understand what had happened and what was happening. It must have been too chilly to go swimming. The leaves on the trees surrounding the fence between our backyard and our neighbors' must have been starting to turn to brown from green. Did I notice then: the cycle of things?

"What will I wear to the funeral?" I remember asking, arms raised laterally for better balance as I kept walking and walking around the shape of the pool.

"Grandma loved that blue dress on you," my mom reminded me.

Now, when I hear newer friends (friends who never knew me as a runner, never witnessed what I did to my body, never participated in it with me) talk about running ("I'm thinking about training for a half marathon!" or "I hate running, but I know it's good for me.") and I say nothing, or nothing much, or nothing true, I start thinking, *This is how you cut yourself out of your own story. This is how the last remaining pieces of the runner and the running body and the races and the injuries turn into nothing but the absence of something.*

In these moments, I tell myself to get familiar with this feeling of losing one's history. After all, when I see my dad, I don't always see the football player he once was. The one so good it got him to college, took him out of Tucker County. In his senior yearbook, in the text beside his image, where they printed each student's plans and dreams for the future, my dad's says, "I want to play football." If it weren't for football, he says, he doesn't know what he would be doing. He was recently inducted into his university's Hall of Fame. But I've never seen him block a body. Never watched him stand on the sideline, something like lightning in his eyes. I'm imagining lightning there—a spark, at least—but maybe his eyes grew cold. Maybe they turned icy. I have to imagine because I wasn't around until he was pulling out of the driveway early in the morning, pulling back in later that evening, getting on with a life that I never realized must have sometimes felt like waking up in the middle of a good, good dream. At least, that's what it sometimes feels like to me. There are so many endings we don't get to see.

There are probably people I would lose touch with if it didn't mean losing touch with the me that I was when I was running, when I was a running body. Isn't acceptance the most devastating step in the grieving process because it is inside a state of acceptance that you risk losing what you have lost? That's to say, in acceptance, you risk the memory of the loss, and as it follows, the losing? When a scar fades, aren't you more likely to forget the injury?

Healing is supposed to be a beautiful thing, but healing requires you to shift your relationship with the past. It requires you to rewrite the story, or at least, the ending. To heal properly you must forget, maybe not the whole thing but parts, certainly. The whole must become hole-y. In this way, healing is its own kind of loss.

After I could no longer use the number of miles I ran that week to form my identity, I turned to injury. I went from the running body to the fractured body because I did not know any other way to be. Did not know how to define myself without the body and its abilities at the very center. Now that the physical injuries have healed, I worry my propensity to keep returning over and over to the points of fracturing—my inability to look away—is connected to the vague notion that maybe, if I do look away, I will have to make myself more than who I was and what I did to my body. I will have to make myself free.

On the other hand, I also worry my propensity to return over and over to the point of fracturing—my inability to look away—is connected to the vague notion that maybe, if I can uncover the precise instant in which I lost the running body, I can set myself back on fire. Burn all this present away so that all that's left is the runner I was supposed to be.

And I also worry, of course, that if I look away, who I was and what I did to my body will turn to nothing in my memory. Or nothing but a hole.

Imagine: You lose something but eventually become so comfortable with the loss that you forget you ever had the thing, and so eventually, this comfort erases the absence, or at least, the presence of the absence—your awareness of it, your ability to see and feel and (at)tend to it—and as it follows, your comfort with the loss erases the state of ever having.

In 2016, at a bar in Laramie, I told a man I had never been slapped and I wanted to be slapped—to experience the feeling—and so he suggested that he might slap me after I take a shot of whiskey. The date had already gone in such a way that I no longer cared how it ended up going. After he slapped me, I looked at my face in the mirror behind the bar and pressed my hand to the red marks on my cheek where his hand had pressed into me. "That wasn't hard enough," I said. "Slap me again."

There was a place inside the running body that turned to something like a well and inside that well existed all of the pain the running body had made. To dwell even briefly inside the well of pain was too much for the self or the soul or the mind or however we might think of such things, and so the self or the soul or the mind would have to leave. It left to keep from getting trapped in the pain. When the self or the soul or the mind goes away—how can I explain what happens inside the body? Language is always failing. It is something like ecstasy but not exactly. It is both more and less than ecstasy. Because it is nothing and everything. Because, for even just moments, the emptiness is filling; the emptiness is whole and complete.

And from this experience: a theory. Deep inside the well of pain is where perfection exists. People are skeptics of perfection because it is simply so hard to get to, to feel, to know. It's easier to dismiss it as delusion. It's harder to admit perfection exists, even harder to admit it exists within us—always there, ready, just in case you muster up the strength to get out of the way. That perfection exists at the precise point where the deepest pain meets the most intense pleasure is what we might call a difficult pill. But difficult as it may be, I know that it is real. I know that it is so real that, for a period of time, it seemed like the only real thing. Perfection is unspeakably pristine. I have tried to capture it in some way here, in this blank space, with this failing language, but with every attempt at capture it eludes me.

At high school track and cross country meets there are often T-shirts for sale. They say things like "Canal Winchester Invitational" on the front and "Pain Is Weakness Leaving the Body" on the back, but I always felt pain as an entering. I felt the body in pain become a body for pain. I tried to make my body a warm place where I could convince the pain to stay and stay and stay. I thought pain was the only pleasure worth having because it was the only pleasure that seemed to lead to freedom. But what did I know about freedom?

Knowing nothing, I turned pain into muse. But I got too greedy. I wanted too much; I (am trying to) take responsibility. I can no longer remember what it feels like. I only know that it *felt*. And now, I have this empty space. The space I made for it to dwell. The space I made in hopes that it would stay. I don't know whether I should keep chasing after it—the perfect inside the pain, or perhaps, on the other side of pain. Either way, the perfect I sometimes felt while running.

Some athletes claim to be addicted to suffering but others reject this. They say, instead, they are addicted to where their suffering may lead. What it might allow them to get out of their body. These people are addicted to winning. But to the ones on the other side, those addicted to suffering, winning is somewhere between terrifying and beside the point. It marks an end to the suffering and to the chase for more suffering, inside which exists the possibility for the kind of pain that feels, as I've tried to describe, baptismal—pure, perfect, purposeful. I should speak, though, less generally. I should admit that up until recently I thought that physical pain might be the only antidote I thought I'd ever need to all my tired metaphysical suffering. I should admit I still sometimes think this way, but I can't, or I won't. Still, I wish I could describe how seductive it feels—at first resisting the pain and then throwing up the door, allowing it to rush in and take and take and take. I suppose some relate the experience to a kind of flow, a kind of harmony. But it never felt that way to me. It felt far more violent, almost fiery. Then, of course, it felt like nothing. There was nothing left to feel, or to say it more precisely, no one left to feel it. The body, finally briefly irresistibly, let free to do its work, make its meaning. Emptied out of what it didn't need. The first page of my journal from 2014 reads, "Now I'm stuck inside this broken body," but even knowing the costs, would I have resisted the sense of freedom I felt from giving my whole self over to something?

The problem with giving something all of you is you can't get all of you back. You're no longer a whole thing. You turned something outside of you into a home and now you have a hole. You discover the trouble with having a body: There are so many things to fill it with but nothing that it can be filled by.

During the first fracturing, a lineman asked me, "Who's the craziest one on your team?" Most of the other football players were finished rotating between the cold and hot tubs and had wrapped tight white towels around their oblique muscles, dripping through the training room back to their locker room, or lingering between the two, flirting with whoever was in between. I had been running on the underwater treadmill for over an hour already, a heavy weight belt strapped tight around my rib cage. I was trying to keep my endurance up without asking the fractured bone to bear the weight of my body on grass, asphalt, concrete. Suspended in a fog of chlorine, I was cranking up the resistance, increasing the power of the waves around my body—kept hard from relentless cross-training, but always at risk of softening. Sweat dripped from my face to neck, mixing with the water. I was paying close attention to the third metatarsal, trying to determine if it had crossed the line between fractured and healing. "What?" I ask, not because I didn't hear him but because I wanted to hear him say the words again. "You know," he said, shouting a little louder over the hum of the machines, "the craziest one?" I smiled through gritted teeth. "Me."

Like any good addict, I used running until it began using me. I suppose this is the other side of freedom—the side that is harder and more dangerous to romanticize. I lost all control is what I mean. In the back of one of those coffee shops that stays open late, in the southeast corner of Portland, I heard a man say hitting bottom saved his life. He said it just like that: "Hitting bottom saved my life." And I heard another man agree and I heard another man say, "I don't know, man. Sometimes it takes all my energy, all day, not to hit somebody."

Once my mileage climbed to numbers even the most elite college programs in the country would consider too high for most of their female athletes, especially those just two years out of high school, I arranged my class schedule to allow for a two-hour nap between my morning workout and afternoon practice. Rick told Juli and I that it's what the pros do, but of course, I already knew. A nap in my schedule meant that no matter when I was waking up, morning or afternoon, my next run was never far away. All I had to do was braid my hair and tie my training shoes, bounce down the three flights of stairs out of Boyd Hall and run easily across West Green to the track, every step shaking sleep out of the running body.

I loved how sleeping after sociology and accounting made 800-meter repeats or 6-mile tempos on the bike path come faster than they would if I had to stay awake, waiting. I loved hearing the soft beep of my GPS watch, beginning to track my distance, pace, calories. I loved the sun or wind or rain or snow on my cheeks, still rosy from sleep. I loved everything about running, being a runner, inhabiting a running body.

Or at least, that's how I remember feeling. We know falling in love changes your brain, but could it have been the same with me and running? Dopamine (euphoria!), adrenaline and norepinephrine (butterflies, heart skipping beats, preoccupation, restlessness, losing sleep like I did that summer, lying awake, dreaming). The brain's pleasure center lights up like a Christmas tree. Do the lights go out eventually? Is that first hit of love ever enough to last, or is sustaining love more about remembering?

I can't remember all the ways I loved running. All I loved about it. I think I probably felt it spreading through every cell of my body. I think even the injuries were like openings where it found more ways of entering. I can still feel all that love somewhere unreachable in me.

But now so many of the scenes come in muddled, muddy—like spikes sinking inches deep in wet ground, legs steering themselves around trees, gritting teeth, head pounding with the effort of trying to forget itself, trying to take the pain, finish line coming into focus before disappearing, air evading chest cavity—and cannot be cleaned. These memories, I think, have slipped from my consciousness in self-defense. But what good does that do when my body remembers everything?

Aside from chasing the perfect inside the pain, I can't pinpoint exactly what else it was (or is) about running. All I know is the only way I have ever known how to feel "the present" as anything more than an abstraction is to go running. To let the miles fold around my body, to give time a break from containing me.

Of course, I have a handful of theories. Like maybe it has something to do with gravity, or the pace of the world spinning and its relationship to the pace of the body running, or the speed of light as compared to the speed of flight between foot strike, or the tide turning. Or the moon. Of course, the moon! Something to do with the way it pulls the water in and out, over and over, and sometimes with a fury we can't even imagine because we don't know—cannot possibly know—what it's like to do the work of the moon only to get outplayed by the sun and all the drama of its setting and rising. The theories are not holding, but this is what I know because this is what I have felt happening: While the body is running the instants do not just stretch but come undone and blur to one long and flat instant of being.

Just after I moved to Laramie, I became preoccupied with the theory of general relativity. I checked out eleven books from the university library and started seven of them before realizing my interests were a bit more specific. I became a little feverish in the face of a certain physical possibility. Something like: If you move faster than the speed of light, you can slow down time. You can open time like a door and move through. As if everything that has ever happened and ever will happen is sitting together in the same room. And you just get to choose.

When actors transform their bodies for a role, do they forget who they are, even just a little bit? I mean, do they get lost in performing inside a body that no longer belongs to them, but to the character? I mean, do they go to a place in which they cannot come fully back? Do they lose something? Some parts of themselves erased to make room for the new? And once the role is over, and the curtain is drawn, per se, do they feel disillusioned, changed in unspeakable ways, confused? Do the parts of themselves that they forced out come back when the character leaves? Or does the character stay, changing them irrevocably? Or, what if, the new character leaves, and the old parts of themselves they shoved out stay gone for good, and all they are left with is a fresh, gaping empty?

RICK WAS ALWAYS talking about building the base. He said if you built it big enough and strong enough, it would never go away, or it would, but it would never go far. He said his body still remembers running 100-mile weeks in his twenties. For example, he would tell us, every summer, when he took advantage of the longer stints of daylight and better weather to run more miles than he did the rest of the year, when he began demanding more from his body, he said he could feel the old miles returning. He could feel his legs answering all the questions that the miles were proposing. The seven or so excess pounds he gained over the winter would drop effortlessly, he would always add. "It's all science," he would tell us. "Your body is remembering."

I believe this is true, and I've read the first chapters of *The Body Keeps the Score*, understanding that it does, but I did not get to the part, if such a part exists, where van der Kolk explains how to prevent our body's memory from transferring from body to body. How do we stop the score from accumulating?

In my dreams, I am often giving birth to babies that are not babies. Or they are babies, but not human ones. They are babies made of cardboard—bloody and crying. Or they are frozen garden gnomes wearing those Halloween masks modeled from the movie *Scream*, except with sharp and jagged teeth. I always recognize the men standing beside my bed at the hospital—from the gas station or the gym—but I never know their names. Not even in the dream.

Aside from the phantom fractures, my body mostly remembers its violent transformation: hunger, sometimes even slight, feels like starving. My body is always on high alert, it seems, watching out for any signs that there will soon be a famine. In the wake of a skipped meal, even if only because I became too busy to tend to it, my body feels on the edge of threat. I become dizzy and shaky and most of all, on the cusp of emotional collapse. When I think about hunger I often think about my first poetry teacher taking one bite of a hard, shiny green apple at the beginning of class one day, then not touching it again until the very end. "All eating is emotional," she told us as she chewed slowly.

When I become hungry I become desperate. It is a state of emergency, a guttural scream. My hunger is like that arcade game. Something about whacking a mole? I tried to destroy it but it kept returning. I once thought of hunger like desire—that it can be both emptying and filling. I thought it was romantic—my body eating itself for lunch and all of that. But now I understand that hunger is nothing like want—it is, instead, need.

And yet, there is something about hunger that is hard to shake. I *want* to feel it sometimes, is what I mean. Because it is a pain that is pleasurable? Now I am thinking, once more, about the ancient Greeks. Plato and his posse. They thought about hunger this way: It is only pleasurable to eat *because* hunger is painful. The conclusion was that pain and pleasure are not separate in the way that good and evil are separate. That, in fact, pain and pleasure are not separate at all. Is there any pleasure without pain? And now, a different question that only sounds the same: Is there any pain without pleasure?

IN EARLY 2016 I booked a ticket to Los Angeles for the Olympic Marathon Trials. I had called Juli to report my latest romantic disappointment—I had not yet learned what my body had tried to teach me. I wanted what he could not or would not give—what I could not, in the first place, receive. After I had exhausted the story and finally asked her how she was doing, she told me how she was feeling about the trials, just a few weeks away. Chris would be racing in hopes of making that summer's Olympic team, and she would not only be spectating, but also hosting his family and friends for an after party in the large house they had rented up in the hills. There was a lot of pressure around the whole thing, a lot of anxiety, but there was also this sharper edge. Running had not been going well for her—small injuries always threatening, control always slipping—and Chris's success seemed to sting. "I want to be there for you," I said, navigating my browser to Expedia. "Plus, Melissa will be there too," I said, choosing the cheapest flight. "And it's so freezing here. I need some sun on my face."

Necessary questions: Did I long to look and look and look at all the running bodies? Did I hope the whole experience might return me to that summer? To all that looking that bonded Juli and I together in Eugene?

Answers: I longed to look. I hoped that looking and looking might pull me back to all those points of no return. I thought I might be able to scatter them around me.

On the day of the race it was eighty degrees. By 10:00 a.m. my face was burning. A drop of sweat made its path from neck down back. My eyes hurt behind my sunglasses because the night before my body refused sleep. On one of the leather couches in the living room of the house Juli and Chris had rented, I laid on my back and stared up at the ceiling. I felt on an edge as I watched Chris and hundreds of other athletes run up and down a stretch of Figueroa. In the late hot morning haze everything was waning and the Olympic Trials Marathon would be starting soon and, I remembered, Chris wasn't supposed to be there. He said that once. Something like: "I'm not supposed to be here. College walk-ons aren't supposed to place in major marathons all over the world. College walk-ons aren't supposed to qualify for the Olympic trials." The race would start soon, though, and he was there. I watched his body as it grew larger when he came closer to me, then smaller as he moved away.

Melissa was a few blocks from the start. The running shoe company she worked for had a promotional tent set up. Juli was somewhere along the course. Once the race began, she would move from point to point, catching glimpses of Chris as he ran by, updating his Twitter feed. Annie, who was a fifth-year senior when Juli and Melissa and I were freshmen, and who was a very fast and accomplished runner and did not destroy or starve her body, and who moved to LA after spending some time pursuing professional running in Eugene, texted me that she found a way into the closed off area with the bleacher seats, where we could watch the racers loop by without moving. I would go off to find her soon, but standing along the street alone, trying not to lean against the temporary plastic fencing, made me feel like I was there on some kind of business—a journalist, maybe. I felt more like a screen than a being—filtering every image of every body through mine, trying not to give any one image, any one body, too much meaning (i.e., trying not to connect, compare, fall into fantasy).

After Chris did not make the Olympic team, I wrapped my arms around his body and felt his razor-edged shoulder bones cutting through me. I pulled away quickly. I had never felt less like a runner, less connected to the world built up around it. I tried not to be surprised or interested in such feelings.

Later that evening, in the backseat of a rental car, I used my eyes to measure the relative radii of Chris's knee cap versus mine versus Juli's. I did this even as a small child—always confused by how much larger my knee caps seemed than the other small children also sitting crisscross applesauce around whatever rug, in whatever room, while whatever teacher read whatever story to us. My body was taking up too much space in the back of the small car. I wanted to apologize. I wasn't supposed to be there—or at least, didn't need to be. I squeezed my legs tighter together, felt my knee caps grinding like teeth.

The plan was to spend a few hours at Chris's party then get a ride downtown where I would join Melissa at a brand-sponsored party. I wore black velvet pants, black sneakers, a sleeveless sweater

I picked up at a vintage store in Laramie and the most expensive piece of clothing I owned, a camel-colored Pendleton cape that my mother had sent me for my birthday. My hair was long and curled loosely and my makeup light—just a couple of dabs of this and that here and there. I could not help but dress that way for parties: a strange mash of who I was and who I hoped I was becoming.

When we got to Chris's party in the hills—I still don't know which hills—I drank two cans of beer in the bathroom and stared at my body in the mirror until I could feel the booze buzzing in my bloodstream. I told myself I was drinking to get all the images of all the running bodies out of my head, but really, I just liked the feeling. Plus, I was frustrated with Juli. Rather than mingling with Chris's family and friends or at least talking to me, she was giving all her attention to two small children. I wanted us to seem cool and mature, but she was taking up the role of babysitter and I was forced to either take up the role with her or mingle on my own. The party collapsed under the weight of my expectations and then I collapsed along with it.

Eventually, someone noticed that we had nearly all of the right people to recreate a photo from years before at Hayward Field in Eugene—from that summer when Juli and I were there racing Junior Nationals. "I don't smile that way anymore," I said when I looked at the original on someone's phone, feeling proud that I had recently started to smile without teeth, realizing it decreased the roundness of my cheeks (an insecurity my mom passed down). After we took the photo, I pulled Juli back inside the house and tried to convince her to come to Melissa's work party with me. She refused, and I started crying. I don't know why I thought she would or even could leave Chris's party. Instead of walking into the party when the car dropped me off I walked away from it, crossed a street, found a spot underneath a bridge and sat there, feeling scared of my tears, the way that they would not stop coming. Soon, Melissa left her party to find me, then we walked back to her hotel room where she held me. "It's okay to not be okay," she kept saying. I kept telling her I did not know why I was crying, and that I know it was not fair to be upset with Juli. Now I think the pain I had been keeping—the pain I had made a home for inside me—was just beginning to get released. Maybe the whole day had forced open the lid. Maybe I was scared I would not be able to close it again.

I've always been bewildered by the way mornings after nights like that tend to feel. It is as though they happened to a different version of me, in a different dimension. I wake up feeling as if I am back in control of myself and my emotions. The sun is shining. Everything looks the same. The puff of the skin around my eyes is the only proof it happened at all.

Waiting at my gate, sober and sleepy, I sensed that I was waiting for the feelings from the night before—or any feelings at all—to come back up to the surface, to once again, start gushing. I felt empty and couldn't remember why I made the trip in the first place. Which delusions was I following?

Throughout the flight I started to understand the trip as, primarily, a kind of testing. I felt empty that morning because the results were not what I had expected, what I had been hoping for: a return. I wanted being at the trials to trigger a flood of memories: running and racing, dreaming and believing. And I wanted those memories to be kerosene on a nearly burned-out fire. I wanted to regain full control over my body so that it might, once more, do away with me. I wanted to get loose and lost over more and more miles, wet feet on wet leaves or hot feet on hot asphalt or flying without remorse down gravelly hills or blistering and callusing and dead nails falling out of their places on toes, sweat-turned-salt stuck on skin, traveling further and further away. I wanted to see if being there and looking at all those running bodies would help me regain the same focus and determination and the rage against flesh I once had. But instead, after watching the running bodies bounce on the starting line, spurred into action by the sound of gun, and after my feet grew tired and sore as I stood around watching, and after listening to the announcers call the names of all the people I would never be or beat, and after trying to slide through the crowd after the race, arms and shoulders rubbing against the racers and their families, and noting, of course, the way their muscles and bones pressed themselves to the surface of their skin, and noting, with a greater degree of surprise, the way I felt almost like a ghost, almost like I was haunting a life I almost lived, after the night and the crying, after all that, I felt nothing. As the plane settled in above the clouds, I began to understand this nothing as an effect of healing. I began to understand that all those tears had released something stored up in me, and that now, the nothing was in their place. Maybe this—this evidence of recovery—should have been thrilling, or at least grounding. Instead it felt like a whole new loss. A betrayal, even. I was mad at myself, at time, at the way, together, we were both moving. I opened my notebook, and for the first time since leaving Athens, started to try to write the story of what I had done to my body.

# IV.

"Isn't he beautiful?" I asked my friend, leaning over the plate of cheese-and-chicken nachos we were sharing. I took a long sip of the lime-green margarita in front of me. Running bodies jumped over steeples on the TV screen above our heads. Through the screen we could see that it was still a sunny day in Eugene, the sky sparkling, but it was getting dark in Laramie. The bodies chasing down and jumping over the steeples (picture extra-large hurdles) were trying to make it to the finals of the US Olympic Track and Field Trials. I was trying to choose the heaviest, most cheese-saturated chip. "He doesn't even look human," she said. Wistful, I chewed quickly and kept my eyes on Evan Jager, a Nike-sponsored steeplechaser with shoulder-length blond hair and long muscles roped around long limbs (picture a ballerina).

The next morning I stayed at the gym for over three hours—pushing, pulling, jumping, forcing. I stayed until I felt hungry, high, buzzing with empty. It was less that watching the trials triggered a response and more that I didn't know what else to do with the energy tequila always seemed to ignite inside my body.

I started feeling sick with something as soon as I got home. The next evening, having hardly left bed all day, lying under the sheets in a NyQuil haze, I found a link to watch more of the Track and Field Trials live. The first heat of the women's 5K prelim was just beginning, and a runner wearing plain black spandex shorts and a plain black racerback top—the uniform of the unsponsored—worked to the front of the long train of bodies. It was early for such a bold move. I braced myself against the voices of the two male analysts calling the race. Soon, they started saying what I knew they would be saying: discounting this woman and her ability.

They said she will be a "nonfactor" once the racers get into the "meat and potatoes" of the race. I could not help but notice her stride appeared ever-so-slightly more labored than many of the other racers, her legs turning ground from the command of her hips, while her torso and arms appear to resist—just a bit—her body's forward progress. Many of the others gliding behind her, a bright stream of professional kits and team uniforms, seem to stride forward with their entire bodies. Every inch of them working in synchronicity to move in the very same direction at the same speed. All flow and flowing.

With a little over a mile to go, my laptop screen gets all pixelated and each running body blurs together. For a few seconds, I see only a multicolored smudge. When the livestream clears, the running bodies have decided it's time to eat. Picture each set of sharp bones as a pair of teeth. The unsponsored woman stumbles along the rail a bit as runner after runner passes her. She gets tangled up in their feast, then disappears from the frame completely. Swallowed. The men calling the race don't mention her again.

With a mile or so to go, the men begin to talk about the youngest athlete in the race—a college freshman. "You can see the very thin and very young-looking Ostrander make her way up through the pack," one says. They compare her running body to the Nike-sponsored Jordan Hasay, who like Ostrander, was a standout on the national running scene from a very young age. The analysts note that Hasay is usually the slightest one in the race. "But just look at how toned her muscles look today. You can see the striation on Jordan, can't you Bill? Compared to her, the young college girl is underdeveloped. A protégé."

By the end of the week, the trials were over, and it was decided who would go to the Olympics in Rio de Janeiro and who would stay home, mending. I woke up and watched post-race interviews in bed, shoveling in a bite of egg then a bite of oatmeal then a long gulp of coffee. With each chew, I felt my illness-induced collarbone prominence fading in defeat. I tried not to think about how beautiful I would be if I lived on nothing but Powerade Zero and saltines.

I watched the interviews all morning. Emily Infeld, Jenny Simpson, Brenda Martinez, Jordan Hasay, Katie Mackey (crying and saying "I'm sorry, I'm sorry."), Abbey D'Agostino (who seemed stoned but I suppose was just very happy), and Shannon Rowbury (cool, calm, angry). In each woman I recognized the kind of possession I once experienced. Looking at them through my screen, I felt taunted by their hollowed cheeks and jutting collarbones. Though I resisted pressing pause, their images still took up a kind of occupancy. For weeks they kept me company; it was like a beautiful haunting.

A couple of months later, Shalane Flanagan finished the Olympic marathon in Rio and almost immediately, a man shoved one of those big network TV microphones in her face.

"How does it feel to finish seventh in the Olympics?" he asked.

Shalane looked directly at the camera. The man seemed very large but only because she seemed very small. He hovered over her body.

"This is not what we dreamed about," she said.

It was the first time three American women had finished in the top ten of an Olympic marathon, the man reminded her.

"I wanted to place higher than seventh," she replied.

The man touched the device planted in his ear, looked down slightly, trying to hear something.

"I'm sorry," he said, looking back up. "It was sixth. You finished sixth."

Shalane released the smallest laugh. "Okay, that's what I thought."

Her depletion appeared total. Her body shriveled as she spoke. Her muscles strained just to keep standing. Visible veins labored to move blood. The man with the microphone seemed to feed on whatever was left of her, the very last scraps. She seemed to refuse to smile—to look pretty or sexy or pleased. For entire seconds the man lingered silently, holding the microphone under her mouth. In those empty seconds, she began to shake very slightly. She gave no thanks and no glory. Not to God or her husband, coach, family, body. The camera cut away from Shalane's hard face, back to the men's race.

AROUND THIS TIME, after I had been living in Laramie for nearly a year, I started to go to the university gym every day. My workouts sometimes lasted two hours. I preferred them grueling. I preferred, even more so, to look around and know I was working harder than any of the men in the gym. I wanted them to wonder who I was, what I was doing. It was the first time since all the injuries that I felt like my body was getting better at something. It reminded me of that summer when I became running body—every day a discovery. I could lift, push, and pull more and more with each passing week. I could jump higher and hang on longer. I was getting strong quickly, and the strength was changing my body.

I also developed a habit of watching fitness YouTubers while I ate breakfast. Most of the women whose videos I watched were training for either powerlifting competitions or bikini competitions, but either way, their videos often showed their intense focus on controlling their food intake. I found this striving for control familiar, comforting. I adopted many of their eating habits like osmosis. Eggs whites, oatmeal with protein powder stirred in, sweet potatoes with kale and lean cuts of meat. Similar to how I was toward the end of my time in college, when I first began to experience the compulsion to eat and eat and eat, and became desperate for any way to regain a sense of control, I allowed myself to eat large portions of food but spent equally large portions of energy controlling what those large portions contained (and did not contain). Still, I was often tormented by an urgent need to eat large portions of the foods I (and the internet) had deemed "bad." On Thursday afternoons, I would often pedal my bike to the co-op in downtown Laramie and fill a basket with nut butters and dried fruit and nut mixes and granola. I would make promises to myself about making it last through the weekend. Then, I would eat it all in a matter of hours, willing my body to do its digestive work before it would be time for old fashioneds at Front Street and whiskey doubles at The Buck. Sometimes, whoever was the most sober would drive everyone else to the all-hours Mexican restaurant on the other side of town. Other times, we would stop at the Loaf and Jug on our walk home for post-bar and pre-bed snacks. I was twenty-three and twenty-four and twenty-five and though I ping-ponged constantly between trying to lose control and trying to control everything, it was the first time I had formed friendships and felt a sense of self-worth that had nothing to do with running—which is partly why I sometimes felt lonely and lost and longing, but also why I often felt like my relative happiness in Laramie was proof that I had gotten away with what I had done to my body.

Maybe it is to give too much away to say my relationship with the gym was more of a brief affair than a long-term, committed type of thing. More like heat lightning than the kind of storm that wakes you up in the middle of the night and lasts until morning. Still, for as long as the brief flash lasted, I loved very much to move heavy weight using my body, by which I mean, doing so provided a sense of purpose, structure, progress, and routine.

It would sometimes scare me—this flashing love. The way the muscles would loosen and the sweat would break through skin. The way my breath would change rhythm. The way I could not, in the middle of a set, think about anything other than moving that particular weight in that particular way. The way I felt like I was carving a new version of myself every session, set, repetition. How I did it all without running.

During my time in the gym, I became especially enamored with deadlifts, at least partly because they were my best lift. I thought about the number of pounds I could pull off the ground nearly as much as I thought about my race times and workout splits and body weight in the years before. I would sometimes do ten sets of ten, which felt like an endurance workout, or something like five sets of three, which felt less familiar, like short sprints. I would tighten my lifting belt and squirt more liquid chalk onto my hands and take a deep breath and pull and pull and pull. I would invest a sense of purpose in every pull. Like I did with my races and workouts as a runner, I would try to convince myself that, at least for the moment, there was nothing else. And sometimes, right after an especially challenging set, I would stumble around dizzy and some thought like, *This is saving me*, would shoot through my bloodstream. Thoughts like this scared me because I wasn't sure I wanted to take part in any kind of saving. I wasn't sure I was ready.

Lifting challenged my premises, revealed holes in my stories. The more I lifted, the more I understood that the mind and body are not divided in the way I previously thought. I could feel my muscles thinking. I noticed that moving weight in particular ways was not about overcoming my mind, but about using it. I didn't have to disappear myself to get the hardest work done—I had to stay very present, actually. Though my relationship with lifting and spending large amounts of time at the gym and disciplining my eating and watching my body change was ultimately a continuation, or at least a variation, of the destructive way of being I had practiced in the years before, lifting heavy weights over and over taught me I did not have to lose my whole self or conquer my mind or leave my body in order to feel that it (my body) was purposeful. It taught me, from time to time, that I could be filled up by something—something like love, like ecstasy—that had nothing to do with running.

Aside from my brother Isaac and my friend Kat, who was also into lifting, I shared my new love with no one. I was embarrassed by it—spending hours at the gym seemed antithetical to the artistic part of me I had come to Laramie to develop. Plus, lifting seemed even more explicitly connected to the desire and possibility to change one's appearance than running seemed. Though, in popular culture, both running and lifting are often explicitly connected to this desire and possibility. At that time, it felt very necessary that I be constantly working to change my appearance but equally as necessary that I try to do so without anyone being privy to the trying. I knew it wasn't good enough to be young and beautiful and thin—knew I had to be all of these things "naturally" (so as not to reveal these conceptions of eternal youth and beauty and thinness as unnatural states of being).

It's also possible that I understood I was ever so slowly turning myself toward recovery, and that I did not talk often or openly about my gym habit because I knew there was a fine line between *This is saving me* and *This is breaking me*. Maybe I did not want to risk setting my habit in language; inviting another physical practice to become part of my identity.

By the fall 2016, less than a year into my lifting regimen, my body was changing so significantly, yet so incrementally that I returned to some of my old ways of measuring. I hardly ever weighed myself at the gym and did not have a scale in my apartment, but I would usually stand in front of my bathroom mirror with my shirt and bra off as I brushed my teeth. I would, like I used to, look over every inch of my body, or at least all the inches the mirror reflected back. Toward the end of the year, my boobs were diminishing and the crater in the center of my chest was, once again, revealing itself, coming to the surface of things. I'd put my pinkie in it and feel that old rush returning. That relief to see proof of the work I was doing. With my finger pressing against skin against bone I'd feel a sense of faith or of the divine. Maybe there is a higher power, I would think—or I would not think this, but I would feel it. With my pinkie in its shallow cave, I craved old cravings.

Sometimes I would pick up my phone to take a picture of the reflection of my body, but after taking the photo, I would delete it immediately. Like that summer more than three years before, I felt a sense of descending—deeper and deeper into the thing. I felt that, after my descent, I would emerge a different person with a different body. I wondered, this time, who will I be?

Being on the way to the gym was becoming my favorite way to be. I would often walk quickly, listening to hip-hop through my headphones, and I would often drink pre-workout in the minutes before I left my apartment. I still don't know what is actually in pre-workout powder, but whatever it was, it moved quick through my blood and left me feeling very warm and all-over itchy. I didn't know how this was supposed to prepare me for workouts, but most of the YouTube fitness influencers I watched took some version of it, so I did too. As I walked, I would feel an almost erotic pull toward the gym—its bright lights and whirring machines and primary-colored weight plates. I would wonder who might be there. I didn't know any of the regulars by name, but I knew their bodies nearly as well as I knew mine. And they knew mine too. We all looked at each other in a way I had never experienced before and haven't since. I still don't know who or what gave us that permission.

I had read somewhere that Karl Marx also thought physical pain was the only antidote to mental suffering. As I walked down Laramie's wide streets, I would think about the pain that lived inside the next couple of hours and feel a wash of relief. I would also curate an inventory of whatever recent temptations I was not able to resist—however many whiskeys, slices of pizza after, fries off a friend's plate, tortilla chips drowned in guacamole and melty cheese. Often, during these, as they say, indulgences, I would remind myself that it was all okay, that I would soon be using this poison as fuel in the gym, that it would all go toward the breaking down and rebuilding of my body.

During this time, I was beginning—but only beginning—to understand the distances between learning in practice and learning in theory. I knew that sweat was not sanctity, or that it was, or that it could be, but not for me, or not in this way. I knew that nothing was really saving me, or at least, not in the way that I needed saving. How could relentlessly and meticulously breaking down muscle fibers only to watch their regrowth be all that different from what I did to my body that summer? Wasn't forcing the body to change itself under the pressure of heavy weight simply a different expression of the same deconstructive tendencies? I knew the answers to both these questions, but I didn't know how to let the answers change my ways of being. I could not yet convince myself not to crave my old cravings. After all, the risky business of deconstruction and reconstruction was still very alluring. Beautiful, even, in that I am the kind of person who finds beauty in what can fool me. Engaged in the process of deconstruction and reconstruction, I felt at ease knowing what my body was up to during sleep. That my body took care of this part of the process on its own felt like all the proof I would ever need. And so, inside the sets and reps, inside the pushing and pulling, inside the triumphant dropping of weight plates, and inside the aching and tearing, it was easy to fool myself into believing I had once again discovered the point of having a body, and as it follows, a purpose for the rest of me.

Though progressing in the gym became a top priority during my years in Wyoming, I had not given up on running. It was always there in the periphery. Not the act of it, I suppose (though I was often racing in my dreams), but what it once meant to me, what I once made of it. I would go out for runs on impulse sometimes, around town or up in the Medicine Bow Mountains, but I never did it consistently. All I can figure is that it hurt too much. Sometimes physically—my fractures left lasting damage, twinges of pain like little hauntings. Sometimes I was too discouraged by the thin air. Up over 7,000 feet even in town, I could never relax into the miles, could never steady my breathing. Sometimes I think it was more of the emotional wound I could not face. Though I no longer mean to separate the wounds by kind—as if the physical were not emotional and the emotional were not physical, as if they weren't all entangled, as if I wasn't all tangled up in them at the same time.

One day, it must have been early spring, the sun shining but the air still crisp, I went to the university track and it was empty. As I walked onto the 400-meter oval, softer than asphalt and concrete, I could not decide if I was grateful or remorseful that no one was there to see whatever was left of the runner I once was. I always admired the spirit of cross country—racing through woods and around fields and across golf courses and up and down hills—but

I respected the track for its uniformity and objectivity. I liked that, if a race went bad, the track resisted any blame—leaving you with nothing and no one to blame but yourself and how you must have went weak.

But back on the track that day, after six laps of warming up to the work, after feeling my tight muscles loosen and release, after feeling my body start to create its own heat, generating it like a machine, I reset my watch and bounced on my toes, pressed start, then took off and tried to unleash something. Smooth and controlled, I was thinking, then when you're ready, let yourself leave.

Though I remained in my body, and though I could not keep smooth and controlled for long before slowing then stopping, I felt like I had lit the littlest of sparks, just from trying.

Another day, I rode my bike away from the gym, pedaling faster and faster and then slower, once I remembered I had nowhere to be, it must have been a Saturday or Sunday, the rain coming down in a slow, lazy way. It had rained with far more purpose earlier that morning, but my bike had been locked up under a tree and so the seat had stayed just fine, just barely damp, and there was something pleasant and inspiring in how undeliberate the rain was doing its falling. And as I slowed my pedals, I noticed a runner moving toward me. I couldn't help but wonder why she was running. I focused on her face as if it would confess something. I wondered if she was running because she liked it. I wondered if running, for her, was a simple thing. Maybe it cleared her mind and helped her sleep. I wondered if running was a tool she was using. I wondered if she was running to maintain her body size, or if she was running in pursuit of its change. I wondered if she was running to erase bits of being—to, as they say, scorch calories. I wondered if, on the other hand, she was just running, and if so, what that might feel like. She shook out her arms a bit as she moved by me on the other side of the street, and though I looked and looked, I couldn't tell why she was running.

I NO LONGER looked like a runner, or how I thought a runner was supposed to look, and I did not think my body, though changing under the force of the weights, had any sort of purpose written up and down its limbs. I figured, when you looked at my body, if you looked at my body, you could think, there is a body that could be used for anything, which to me was basically the same as, there is a body that can be used for nothing. I was still drawn to bodies distinct with purpose—had internalized the notion that beauty and purpose were nearly synonymous. Ballerinas, lineman, the ranchers who passed through town on the weekends. I understood the problem with my way of thinking about purpose, ability, beauty. I knew it was not something to speak about openly unless it was within the frame of critique. And I knew it was unbecoming to think so much about my body—especially now that I had no real reason to do so, no scholarship that depended on such a solipsistic way of being. I was beginning to know better, but all my new knowings slammed right up against the walls of my old ones. "What are you training for?" people at the gym would sometimes ask me. "Nothing," I had to say.

Sometimes, when I stood in front of the small mirror above my bathroom sink and took pictures of my body, it felt like I did it in an attempt to multiply. Like here is my body and here is an image of my body in the mirror and here is the image of the image of my body in the mirror. Sometimes, though, it felt like I did it in an attempt to simulate an erasing. Because after I would take my fingers and pinch the screen here and there to more closely examine "trouble spots," I would delete the images—quickly and cleanly and without thinking. And sometimes I think staring at the images of my body was a sort of intellectual attempt to make my body mean less, mean nothing. Like how if you repeat a word too many times, the sounds distort and become meaningless, arbitrary, and floating. Like perhaps I could undo my body's signification, all that it meant to me.

By this time, when I was twenty-three and twenty-four and twenty-five and living in Wyoming, when it had been over three years since that summer—that summer when I had gotten myself wrapped up in starving—the notion that you should feel positive toward your body no matter your body, and that you should not compare it to other bodies surrounding you in real life or on Instagram, had gone mainstream. Alternatively, the notion that you don't need to feel positive toward your body but instead should accept it as is and work toward a feeling of neutrality toward the way it looks and what it can do was gaining in popularity. I was aware of both of these schools of thought. I was also aware of the ways in which words like "diet" were being traded out for words like "lifestyle." From my view, cultural expectations and pressures around appearance and ability had not changed, it was just that now there was the added pressure to posture as if I had no interest in changing my body to better fit those expectations.

Movements and frameworks like anti-diet, fat positivity, and Health at Every Size were out there, but I had not yet come across them. In activist and academic spaces, there had, for a long time, been discourses percolating around the connections between racism, classism, healthism, ableism, body size discrimination, and homophobia—how all of this was part and parcel of white supremacy, heteronormativity, capitalism, patriarchy. I was not yet aware of these conversations, and though I was aware of the ways my privilege extended far beyond my whiteness—that I had always received unearned advantages because of the ways my appearance and abilities aligned with cultural norms produced and reinforced by white supremacy—I was just beginning to understand the costs, just beginning to understand that part of the privilege itself would be never fully understanding the costs, never feeling their implications on my body. That's why I was able to spend all this time in the space between learning and unlearning, knowing and understanding, and between understanding and doing things differently. I struggled against moving beyond my preoccupation with my body even though I knew I needed to if I ever wanted my growing political consciousness to become porous, to extend beyond my individual troubling.

Knowing this, I still could not find the lines between chasing pleasure and chasing pain, chasing a feeling and chasing a twisted fantasy. I could tell myself over and over again that my workout routine and disciplined eating had nothing to do with appearance, or even performance, that I only did it for mental well-being or as a healthy release of energy, but no matter how many times I told myself these things, and no matter what degree of truth my self-talk held, I could no longer trust myself.

I started to wonder if body trouble works the same as the muscle memory Rick was always referencing. I wondered if it, like memory, was always there, willing and ready. I no longer consciously believed that the worth of my body or anyone else's had anything to do with the work our bodies could or could not do, and I no longer consciously believed the worth of my body or anyone else's had anything to do with what our bodies looked like, and I no longer consciously believed who I was had anything to do with how fast I had once raced a 10K or 5K or 15-mile long run on Sunday morning, and I was actively trying to surrender all the lenses and metrics that had previously brought such order and purpose and comfort to me, but still, I could not keep my eyes from noticing the prominence of collarbone, the knob at the top of shoulder, the ridges down the center of breastbone. And I could not keep my eyes from noticing all the bodies surrounding.

On the third floor of the university gym there was a mirror-lined studio with shiny wood floors and a stack of big blue mats and multicolored medicine balls and large boxes made for jumping and free weights. Because of the room's private and secluded nature, it stayed occupied almost exclusively by women working out by themselves or in small groups, murmuring little bits of encouragement to one another and tightening ponytails and adjusting high-waisted spandex pants and catching glimpses of their bodies from unique angles, angles bathroom mirrors could not provide. Sometimes at the end of my lifting workouts on the main floor of the gym I liked to go into this room and stack a few of the large boxes on top of each other so that I could jump on top of them over and over again. I preferred the room quiet and dark and empty while I jumped down and up, back down and back up. I liked the freedom to fail a jump or two—knees and hands slamming on top of the box or down on the floor—without anyone asking if I was okay, but mostly I liked to be alone so that my body was the only body in the room. This was the only sure way I had found to prevent myself from comparing my body to other bodies.

One afternoon there were three women in the room and they were playing loud pop music from one of their phones and each one was using her own box to perform various exercises I recognized as core-strengthening and leg-sculpting. Because of this, my box supply was limited in such a way that made it impossible to stack the remaining boxes at a height that would be appropriately challenging for my up and down jumping. Instead, I grabbed one of the jump ropes hanging along the wall and did ten sets of one hundred jumps in a fury. As I jumped, I noticed that I was starting to feel high on something that could be mistaken for endorphins but because I was starting to cozy up to myself and my tendencies, I knew I was in fact high on how it seemed like maybe the women were periodically looking over at me and my body jumping and maybe comparing my body to theirs and because of the results of this comparison, feeling their own body trouble rising to a boil.

I finished with the rope and the jumping and grabbed a couple heavy kettlebells and did a couple of sets of step-ups on one of the boxes left available to me. I began to sense that the women weren't going to be done with the boxes anytime soon. I began to sense, even more so, that they had not been noticing me, or comparing my body to theirs, or feeling their own body trouble rising. It seemed just as likely that I had been the one filling the room with its body trouble, troubles, troubling—and that if I did not leave, it might keep spreading.

I walked down the gym's steps and into the women's locker room, averting my eyes. I grabbed my things and moved outside as fast as I could. I walked home slowly and tried to focus on the trees, how the thickness and sturdiness of their trunks seemed related to the spread and growth of their branches and leaves.

I knew enough at this point to stop weighing my body. I could no longer contain the knowledge of the numbers. I wanted the numbers to have less—to have nothing—to do with me. When I saw a scale—tucked in the corner of a locker room or across from a toilet in a friend's bathroom—I knew to look away immediately—to not let my eyes linger on the potentiality. But then, there was the fact of the unopened box in the corner of my closet. Inside the box was a scale Facebook advertised to me. One of the fitness YouTubers I still followed, even after I had mostly shaken my fitness YouTube habit, also advertised the scale on her videos, and I remembered her sharing a discount code for 50 percent off. The scale measured many things. It measured body weight and body fat percentage and muscle mass and more. It was late at night and I had bought the scale very quickly. It felt as if I did it without thinking, but I was thinking, wasn't I? The next morning I realized the mistake I had made, and I emailed the company that made the scale to see if I could please cancel my order. I asked that they stop processing the order, to keep it from shipping. Please, I was asking, don't send this weapon to me. But this whole thing—the ordering and regretting and emailing—all happened over the Thanksgiving holiday and by the time my email was received by customer service, it was too late. The package, they told me, had been released. It was on its way to me. My best option, they said, was to open the box once I received it, find the return label and place it on the outside. Then, I could simply close the box back up with any sort of sturdy tape and drop it off at UPS at my earliest convenience. They assured me I would receive a full refund, minus the cost of shipping, in about a week. But I couldn't open the package to retrieve the return label. It was too risky. Because I could no longer gamble with knowing such numbers, such things about my body, I deleted the emails, shoved the scale away. Though, I often felt its presence there. Not that it haunted me, necessarily, but that it reminded me of all the ways I could not keep from haunting myself.

The winters in Laramie are very long. They usually descend by October and don't lift until at least May. Often, the roads in and out of town completely shut down. When the snow falls heavy and hard enough, there is simply no way out.

As a child, my Grandma Sue's husband, who we called Grandpa Dean, put me in a small wooden trunk during a game of hide-and-seek with my cousin and siblings. When he first shut the lid, I felt fine. "You're going to win," he whispered, then stacked a pile of my grandma's wool blankets back on top of the trunk. The silence settled around my body. Then I heard my sister's footsteps and voice as if I were underwater. Then I realized I couldn't breathe. Then I kicked and screamed. I shifted my weight; I felt that the trunk was doing a violence to me.

During winters in Laramie, I often felt this creep of space closing. My studio apartment was small, and my landlord covered the windows in Saran Wrap to keep the heat in. Usually getting out of it was enough to remind me that, in fact, there was quite enough air to breathe, even if it was very cold and very thin. Still, as soon as spring broke, I gassed up the little red Corolla my parents had bought me when I was seventeen and drove south out of town, toward the state line where Wyoming becomes Colorado and Colorado becomes Wyoming. I put the window down and tried to remember the humidity—the way its thickness holds the body. Even though it made summer training harder, and everything else harder for that matter, I often missed its dense caress. Laramie's high altitude and dry air, on the other hand, usually felt more like trying to run through a wall that no one else could see. I could never figure out how to run with it, rather than against it. I understood the land called Laramie was not mine in a way I never quite did back east, in the places where I grew up. One of my closest friends in Laramie ran regularly and said the altitude never bothered her—not even the first time she went running. *It's because she's skinnier than me*, I could never keep myself from thinking.

Sometimes I would slide down deep into the old bathtub in my apartment and wonder over my body. I knew that baths were this way for me—that I could not take one without engaging the sort of bodily attending that I had grown tired of but not out of. Sometimes I would think, *I can't help it*. Other times I would wonder if I was even trying. My eyes would linger on the palette of bruises running up and down my shin bones. There were faint green and blue bruises, light brown bruises, reddish bruises that were more of a rub, and two twinning bruises of a deep purple right in the center of both shins. There was a scar running up my left one, and I was glad that it was likely there to stay. I thought of these bruises and scars as barbell hickeys—places where the steel marked its territory, proof of all the work I was doing.

Next, I would notice my shoulders and worry an old worry over their wideness. Then I would raise my hands out of the water and trace my fingers along the lines of my deltoids. One by one, I would straighten my arms and slowly trace my triceps, pressing into the muscle to measure its hardness. I would hold my right bicep in the palm of my left hand and tighten my entire arm and feel the muscle expand. I would straighten the arm and place my fingers in the space just under the bicep where my flesh caved. I would search for the pretty blue vein that rose out of my forearm at the gym a few hours ago, but it would always be lying quietly once again under skin. I would run a finger from the base of my neck down the center of my chest where there was once a vein of the most incredible cerulean. I would remember how one of the guys on the team pointed to it and said, "That's crazy Pife," and how I had looked at it and ran my finger down it that very same way and said, "I know," unable to keep myself from smiling.

I would arch my back and watch my stomach and ribs rise out of the water. I would feel for the pectoral muscles at the top of my chest, checking to see if they were sore from all the push-ups I had done the day before. Satisfied, I would turn my attention once more to my shins and press deeply into the bruises and watch the skin turn pale. Without much thought I would start to think, *You are the strongest you've ever been*, and then with even less thought, I would wonder if I should try to get "really lean," to eat less fruit, to limit the body to half a sweet potato at dinner, to decrease my intake of carbs using one of those food-tracking apps. With even less thought, I would imagine how I might look if I were leaner. I would accidentally let the wondering fascinate me. I would begin to calculate how much weight I should lose. I would remember the scale in the closet. I would plan to get out of the bath and take it out and weigh my body. That's when I would always catch myself, and sink my head all the way under the lukewarm water and while I was under there, I would remind and remind and remind myself that just because one can change their body does not mean one should always be trying.

In the bedroom I would let my towel drop to the floor. Standing in front of the mirror that sat on top of the old dresser that came with the apartment, I would stretch my arms up to the ceiling and look at my ribs. I would try to hate the appearance of them, but I still loved it, didn't I? I bet I still loved how, with my arms up like that, the ribs looked like claws clutching the rest of my torso. Now I wonder what it was about seeing my bones that way. I wonder if it was more habit or more sickness or if, as I suspect, there is no difference.

At a café in town, I scooted my chair back and announced that I was going to the bathroom. "Don't you love the mirror here?" asked a friend. I knew exactly what she meant and quickly agreed: "Yes, it makes me feel so skinny." I didn't tell her that before I left the bathroom and returned to the table, I always lifted up my shirt and looked at the image of my instantly narrower waist, and although I knew the image was doing a certain harm to me, I could not stop looking. The mirror could not be true, and yet, I could not stop looking. Could not stop wanting to believe in what the mirror was communicating. What am I if not what I see? I hated that question, I was becoming wiser than that question, and yet I kept asking it anyway. To spend so much time looking, I knew, was a twisted luxury. I worried I was always trying to understand, but never the right things.

One lonely night, when I ended up at Walmart, the fluorescents offering something like company, I ended up buying one of those flimsy full-length mirrors from one of the center aisles. I didn't go there intending to buy such a thing. It was the last product I picked up on my way to the self-checkout register because I didn't want to see anyone I knew while clutching an object of such vanity. (Looking is a shameful, indulgent activity.) I thought this was paranoia until, on my way to where I knew the mirrors would be (could maybe feel my image beckoning), I passed a man who, from time to time, said things like, "Hey!" and "What's up?" and "You're getting some guns on you," to me at the gym. And so I chose the mirror quickly and calculated where this man might be in the huge, overbearing store, based on where I had last passed his body and the direction in which he was going as we traded our stunted greetings, he stutter-stepping a bit then correcting as my body showed no signs of stopping for a chat. I decided quickly to take the most dangerous, yet direct route to the self-checkout machines and rang up my things and slid my card with a fervor I hadn't displayed towards anything else all week. Walking across the frozen parking lot, my flimsy full-length mirror under my arm, my heart beat as if I had stolen something, but I hadn't stolen anything. The only crime I had committed was a slippage of the mind. I was slowly becoming less of a fool about these things, but lately I was slipping frequently (the scale, the bath), thinking: I can do this, I'm better than I used to be. I got the mirror home and leaned it against a wall in my bedroom and could not help but notice the way it brightened the space, and could not help but notice that no matter where I went in the small apartment, I could hardly escape the image of my body reflecting. And I knew this thin mirror, with its against-the-wall lean, was distorting the width of my body. I knew the image of my body reflecting was more fantasy than reality, but I pretended maybe that wasn't so. I lifted up my shirt and could not help but like the lie the mirror was telling.

Looking in the mirror at the running body felt like looking at something other than me. This hard, sharp thing. I would press my fingers into it, as if investigating. The running body uncovered parts of me I could not know I would spend all this time trying to un-touch and un-see. Touching the running body was like touching something I knew I could never be, but I was, somehow, impossibly.

There was a guy I saw nearly every day at the gym. He wore his baseball hat forward and low. His eyes lingered inside its shadow. We had only held eye contact for half a second at most. His eyes could have been hazel or brown, I didn't know. But I did have a favorite thing about him. It was how he kept his T-shirt on until about halfway through his workout, then took it off the same exact way my first high school boyfriend always took his shirt off before going down on me, reaching both arms up and back over his head, pulling from the fabric around his shoulders. I got no pleasure from any of the ways he touched me, but I appreciated the gesture of offering up more of his body before I offered more of mine to him. I also liked how this man—the one I saw nearly every day at the gym—wore cut-off T-shirts underneath his top T-shirt. I didn't understand the logic behind this practice, but I liked it anyway because the cut-off shirts were chopped in such a way that they revealed a great deal of his torso. The cut-offs were more of a gesture toward clothing than clothing itself. He had a few of these chopped-up items in rotation, but each of them was equally worn and faded. Each of them looked like they had been washed so many times that the sweat was baked in instead of wrung out. I often strained to make out what they said on the front and back, hoping to find something out about him, like where he went to high school or what sports he had played. I never could read them though; this man revealed no identity, only body. I think that I liked it this way. If I didn't know his name, his name could be anything.

I told myself I never noticed him until I felt his eyes on me as I was braiding my hair on the way to a treadmill one morning. I was planning to run a mile as a warmup before I started pulling and pushing. As we walked by each other he took off his hat and scratched the back of his head then set the hat back on top of his head and pushed it down from the top then straightened and settled it from the bill. It seemed like something a cowboy in a Western would do. But while he did it, he looked at me. When I met his gaze, he smiled just slightly. I looked away quickly; my body lit up with something. Seconds later, once I was standing on the treadmill and he had passed by, I looked over my shoulder and he was looking over his too. There was another small smile. That was it, really, but I spent the rest of the day imagining our first conversation—what he would say to me and what I would say back, how his voice might sound, if he was a graduate student too, what he was studying. I took careful note of what I was wearing, assuming it must be what he liked: tight, black clothing. I wondered if he was one of those guys who loved to watch the process of a woman getting ready, and if the sight of me braiding my hair was just enough to get him going.

Sometimes there would be more looking and smiling, and often I could feel his eyes on me in the middle of my sets. I figured all our looking must be adding up to something. A few weeks later, I saw him standing outside a bar where I was sitting, incredibly drunk, if you really want to know, and I thought we made eye contact, and I thought something like, *This is it, he's going to come in here and make good on his looking*, but the thick and steamy glass dividing the distance between our bodies must have been fooling me, and he must not have seen me or he must have been looking at someone else or have been looking at nothing or, more likely, he must have wanted nothing more than the looking, because he and his friends never came inside, and I didn't see him again until we were both at the gym the next morning.

I looked at him as he set a heavily loaded bar back on one of the squat racks that lined the gym's main floor. I looked at him stretch out his back and bend briefly down to his toes then crouch down on his heels and rest there for a few seconds. I looked at his shadowed eyes looking in the mirror. I looked at him look at him. From several feet away, resting on the end of a flat bench between sets, I looked and looked and I imagined what it might be like to have his body. I rubbed my hands up and down my arms, trying to feel his arms instead. I flexed my arms just slightly. I look at the tiny hard muscles coming out of the sides of his back in his cut-off shirt as he lifted the barbell off the rack. I twisted and turned my torso, trying to see those tiny hard muscles organize my own back. I looked at his ass as he settled into the bottom of his squat. I tried to imagine mine as hard as his. In the long mirror that lined the gym's walls, I looked at both his and my body at the same time. In the mirror, his body appeared closer than it was in reality. In reality, his body was out of reach.

I never understood what all our looking meant. All I can figure is that his first smile and look was a kind of offer, which I accepted by returning the smile and look, and that with each subsequent look, we renewed the contract. Sometimes, though, I was only looking as a means of control—if I felt him looking at me and I didn't want him to be, I would look back so that he would look away, as was part of our agreement, it seemed. Other times I looked because he was what I wanted to see.

My favorite thing about the running body wasn't that it was so small, but that it was so hard. As hard as Aaron's body. As hard as any man's I had ever seen. When I was a little girl, my dad would say, "Show them how you can flex," at family cookouts and parties, and on cue I would tighten my leg muscles the way he had taught me. As I began hardening into the running body, my dad looked at me and said, "You're never going to look like Aaron." I had just turned down a piece of barbecued meat. It took a long time to understand my dad had said this in concern—he wasn't challenging me. A few months after, back at school, I asked Aaron to leave the lights on as we started undressing. Carefully, I compared muscle to muscle and bone to bone. I won, is what I was thinking.

The bones of our hips and shoulders and torsos—stretching out against skin, pressing. Aside from the miles we covered together, this is what I remember most about me and Aaron. The way I watched our bones in his bedroom. For years after, I told myself the story this way: He watched me waste away. He only said subtle things.

"You should get the fries."

"You should eat the ice cream."

But now I understand what I had interpreted as subtle was direct, and like a whole lot of other people, he was trying to offer a kind of help I was not willing to receive.

When I returned to campus after that summer, that summer that turned me running body, our athletic trainer asked me if I was getting my period regularly and I said usually. After the first fracture, our team doctor asked me if I was getting my period regularly and

I said usually. After the second fracture, an endocrinologist asked me if I was getting my period regularly and I said usually.

"It's not like you have to worry about the condom breaking," I said once to Aaron, when my period first went away. It stayed that way—gone—for the next two years. But I lied to the people who may have cared, who may have intervened, because I knew lying was the surest way to ensure no one forced me to eat more, run less. I knew what my missed period meant. I had heard of amenorrhea and the female athlete triad: loss of period, not enough food for the training amount or intensity, decreased bone density. I don't know if I understood the costs but thought I was invincible (that I would not have to pay), or if I knew I would have to pay but thought that it (the faster times, the higher places) would be worth any eventual costs (the fractures, the osteopenia, the endings). I don't know if, on the other hand, the costs were lost on me—lost inside the well I had dug for myself, then fallen into, unable to claw out, unable to let anyone help me. It's likely that it was a combination of all these things. I wish I could say with certainty that if I had understood the costs, I would have done things differently. But I can't say that, or much of anything about that time, with certainty. I think I was just sick, is what I mean.

In Laramie, Saturdays and Sundays often brought nostalgia and melancholy. All day, I would feel like I was waiting for something. This sense of waiting was especially pressing during the fall (thankfully brief in Wyoming) when it looked and smelled like cross country season. Then it would get especially pressing again in the spring when it would look and smell like running laps around and around the track. All day, I would think: You're supposed to be racing. But I wasn't, not really. And yet, I would feel tight and tangled inside pre-race energy. I longed for the pain and the chase. I longed, even more, for the lightness and freedom of a long post-race cooldown with Melissa and Juli. Then the sense of muscles growing sore and stiff on the van or bus back to Athens County—how, along with the soreness and stiffness came the assurance that there was no more work to do until morning; how my hunger felt earned, whole body emptied.

More than the busy weekdays filled with workshops and teaching and writing and reading, the weekends were troublesome because they reminded me that I had not yet found a real purpose for my body. I could go to the gym, but I couldn't stay there all day, all weekend. And even if I stayed for a long time, as long as I could, it wouldn't feel the same. I thought this was mostly because I missed the thrill and satisfaction of racing—how all my anticipation got left suspended in a state of rising action, or worse, anti-climax—but now I wonder if it also had to do with how much I missed being on a team, how it felt to be surrounded by a group of people all working toward the same thing.

At some point, I started trying to embrace all the ways I was feeling. I started trying to manufacture a sense of lostness in familiar places. I stayed up late and fell in love with my longing. And in the morning when I felt nothing, I called it an epiphany. I thought I felt most myself when I was drinking—somewhere along the edge of buzzing. Now it seems more likely that it simply felt good to loosen my thinking.

Sober, I would imagine my body as an island. Surrounded with water on all sides. Then, on one fine day, I would imagine my island body floating away. It sounds suicidal, but I don't think it was. I think, instead, I was slowly becoming interested in where I might one day be going.

I longed to say "I love you" while I laid awake in my empty room. I wanted to remember the way the words collapse. How, when said together, they have no edges. I wanted to feel my top row of teeth scrape against my bottom lip for the brief instant between love and you. I wanted to know the shape my mouth took when I addressed you. Instead, I said nothing. I laid inside the longing. I wondered, but did not ask, if anyone else imagined plucking out their organs one by one until they were lighter than they ever dreamed.

# V.

BACK IN COLLEGE, most of the guys on the men's team called one of my teammates on the women's team "FUPA." FUPA means "fat upper pubic area," in case you have, up until this point, been lucky enough not to know. Once when I was back in Ohio around the winter holidays after I had graduated college, I went out with a group of the guys who were living and working in Columbus. One of them proudly showed me an image on his phone. As he pulled it up, a few of the others stood around him, giggling. The image showed two photos of one of my previous teammates, a different woman than the one they called "FUPA," screenshot from Instagram and collaged to appear side by side. On the left was a photo of my teammate during heavy loads of training and restricted eating. On the right was a photo of her after we had graduated and she took a break from running.

You won't be surprised, will you, if I say that even though this whole thing—the name calling, the screenshotting—turns my blood to boil now, back then, standing in that bar with those people, I was relieved? I thought it meant they weren't saying or doing those things about me.

Stretched out on separate couches, I stayed awake until the sun started rising with the man who had pulled up the image on his phone. We talked about how strange it was to live inside our tattered bodies. How we felt so much older than we were. How we missed running and running and running. "We should get some sleep," we both started saying. Then we talked vaguely about what I had done to my body. "This is the hottest weight you've ever been," he said before we finally fell asleep. "Don't ever go back to being that skinny."

I still believe I did what I did to my body because I wanted to be faster, place higher, achieve more. I also wanted to "look more like a runner." I thought that looking more like a runner was a prerequisite to those wants (speed over distance) that felt like needs. As I disciplined myself down, as I wasted away, I became a spectator of my body. The way my body looked became even more entangled with what it could do. I did not just become very hard, I also became very fast—faster than I had ever been before, with better form and greater endurance. For a long time, I understood this to mean I had no choice but to do what I did to my body.

After I was no longer able to use hard workouts and races as a way to measure whether or not my body was "where it needed to be," which is a phrase I peppered throughout my running log as a code for "thin enough" or "fit enough" (at the time, I did not distinguish between the two), I noticed I started to rely more on the gaze of men. More than I ever had before, I started to try to see myself through their eyes, and because of this, my vision got even more blurry.

For example, a guy I had never met looked at my legs for at least five seconds before his eyes drifted dutifully up to my face. After he looked away, I decided the exchange was proof of something. I wanted to live inside his gaze, make a home there, room enough for all of me.

For months, this became our routine. The looking, then looking away. Our relationship became similar to my relationship with the man in the cut-off shirts from the gym, but it felt different, for some reason beyond me. Though we never spoke, I thought I might have been in love with him until I realized I was only in love with what I wanted him to see.

For another example, I just noticed an attractive man at the bar where I am writing. When his date got up to go to the bathroom, I waited with yearning to see if he would look up to make eye contact with me and when he did I felt satisfied, but then, when he looked away before I did, as if he didn't mean to look up at me at all, I felt sunk and buried.

Desire for another, back when I was in my early-twenties, so often felt inextricably tangled up with the desire to be desired by who I was purporting to desire.

While visiting Melissa in Seattle I ended up going home

with one of her new Seattle friends. In the morning I told myself I was letting him have my body because I knew he would not keep it. "I hate you," I kept saying and he kept smiling and saying, "I know, I know." I wanted to accuse him of not knowing anything about me but his sweatpants were shrugging themselves down my legs and I accused him of nothing. "What are you thinking about?" he asked, and I told myself I said nothing because to say something would be to offer up my mind. Instead, I took one of his fingers and put them in my mouth and waited for him to tell me how it felt and he told me it felt good. "What are you thinking about?" I asked him after his finger exited my mouth and he said nothing too but he said it like this, "I'm thinking about you."

I wondered but didn't ask if my performance the night before was satisfactory. I sensed, anyway, there would be another opportunity. I looked at the shoes lined up neatly around his room and remembered his hand on my thigh under the table where no else could see. I remembered how he kept calling me "Em." He called me "Em" over and over and over again, just like he knew me. I remembered grabbing that little white candle from the center of the table and looking at him and putting my finger in the flame and laughing hysterically. "Does this work for girls too?" the man asked, putting my finger in his mouth and sucking. I told him I couldn't speak for all girls, but that it wasn't doing anything for me. "Do you want to fuck or what?" he eventually asked, and I noticed the gray of the sky outside his window and how the sunlight was trying to come through and the way the fitted sheet had lost contact with its corner of the mattress and I said, "I don't know."

In Columbus during the holiday break, the morning after our team's annual alumni Christmas party—"Krunkmas," it's called—I heard the shower running. I felt disappointed in myself for how I responded when, minutes before, he nudged me. "Shower?" this man who I wanted to love me asked. "I don't have any clean clothes," I said, declining. When he came out, fully dressed in his clothes from the night before but now damp and shiny, I was laying flat on the edge of the bed, my feet dangling, and he spread himself on top of me in a way I found troublingly endearing. It was partly troubling because I liked it so much—the feeling of him suffocating me. But even more so, I was troubled with knowing I would never do the same to him, or anyone else—lay down the full weight of me. What if they could not bear it? With my oxygen supply cut off, I flashed to just after the injuries and the losses (of running body, plans, dreams), and how for the next two years, when I was twenty-one and twenty-two and living in New York City, I wouldn't even allow myself to desire another body, I so disavowed my own. When he put his hands on the bed, shifted his weight, and pushed up off me, I felt sadness at an unspeakably high frequency.

Another night, back in Laramie, after the date with the man who slapped me. "Do you have a condom?" I asked, mostly because I wanted the words to jam some space between our bodies. Mostly because if I pulled away to ask the question, he would have to pull away to answer me. Truly, I didn't care to proceed but I had spent the whole day twisted inside my own thinking and I was happy to be doing something useful with my body. "I'm so into everything you've got going on," he said. I told him he didn't know what I had going on, but I said it in the playful way I knew I was supposed to. I had no interest in him but we had come back to my apartment after our drink-filled date and I didn't know what to say to get him to go away. "We'll go to my place and get a condom in the morning," he said as he fell asleep, crowding me.

Out again in Columbus, during a trip home to visit my family. I, a little drunk, leaned across the two men sitting in the backseat of a car with me. "Tell me what you guys are talking about," I said. "I want to be in the bro club." They told me I could not be in the club, and when the car pulled up to their house and they and I and a couple of my friends from high school got out, the tallest one motioned for me to come with him toward the stairwell that led to his bedroom. I sat down at the rolling chair underneath his desk as he asked me if I wanted to watch something. "Not really," I said, as he swung me around in the chair and put his tongue straight down my throat. "I thought we were bros," I said, pulling away and laughing, grateful to the chair for its generous lean. He pointed at the door and told me to leave.

Then, when I was twenty-five, sitting across from a man who—my instincts were trying to tell me—I would be sitting across from for a long time. Around a bonfire in the backyard of a bar in Laramie, the man was telling me a story about his mother, who I would meet and love instantly, but I was not listening, or I was, but not fully. Instead, I was thinking in concentric circles around the absence of language this man had so far made about my body, and I was thinking, too, about how much I wanted to sleep with him because then, I reasoned, he would definitely say something—he would definitely let me in on what he sees when he sees me. Because even when sex was about love, or something getting near it, the moments right afterward so often seemed to be about affirming the work of the involved bodies.

It was once easier for me to rest in certain casualties. Explanations like: All of my coaches were men and proving my worth to them became very important to my well-being, and so without the opportunity to do so, I turned and kept turning to men I knew and men I didn't know. Or like: Running and racing supplied me with a near-constant flow of external validation, and once I could do neither no longer, or at least neither well, I had to learn how to supply myself with validation, but this took a long time, so in the interim, I went seeking. Or like: Sport did violence to me, and even more than that, I used sport to do violence to myself, and once I no longer had access to sport and its promises, all I had was my broken body and my broken heart and it turns out that sport didn't teach me the first thing about real healing. Or something simple and true: I wanted to prove my body was worth something. Now I understand these explanations as not necessarily untrue, but too simple and clean. Causality erases part of the story, and the story already erases part of the reality. How, anyway, do you build something whole out of a series of fracturing? This was never going to be a story; it was always going to be a scratching, a clawing.

I have trouble recalling books I've just read and movies I've just seen. My Grandma Sue died less than twenty years ago, but I have so few memories of her alive and moving. Soon, I worry I will only be able to recall her through photographs, like bread crumb droppings back to the woman she used to be. I leave my keys in doors, forget my grocery list on the counter, miss my closest friends' birthdays. I made a five-year plan for my life five years ago but I can't remember what my plans were, how or if they have panned out. Despite all this memorial loss and losing, all the ways my memory functions like a screen door left open and swinging, I remember every word anyone has ever said to me about my body, and I try to imagine what it would be like if no one ever said anything to me about it again, and I'll tell you this: I don't know if it would cure or kill me.

Penny told me she feels her most beautiful when she is stressed for long periods of time and cannot eat. "Wearing that uniform made me so aware of every pinch of fat on my body. Do you remember lining up for your first college race? Everyone was so skinny. The abnormal became normal. It's all we were seeing," she said over the phone, after one of us recalled the uniforms we wore during races in college: bikini-like bottoms and a tight, cropped tank-top singlet. "I wish I could walk by a mirror without looking at my body," she added. "I bet I haven't done that since high school."

My sister skips long weekends spent visiting our extended family over the holidays because an uncle cannot help but make commentary about her body. A younger cousin gets teased for her round face and stomach.

Kat starts purging again. Kat starts wearing crop tops and spandex shorts again.

Melissa says, frustratedly, that she looks pregnant in one of her engagement photographs. We recall that time at a college party when a senior on the men's team said, "If you could just combine Melissa's tits and Emily's ass, you'd have the perfect body."

I recently showed my parents a photograph of them taken over thirty years ago. They had their arms around each other and they were standing in front of a waterfall, grinning widely, barely twenty. My dad pointed to the image of my mom's body.

"Look how tiny you were," my dad said. "You were smaller than Emily."

"I felt so fat that day," my mom said after she finished sighing.

Sometimes I close my eyes and move my mouth silently over the words, "I have more to offer than my body." Sometimes I can be right on the edge of believing when I remember the problem, in the first place, is that it's not really up to me.

There's a scene in *Mad Men* where Joan looks Peggy up and down, her outfit loose and frumpy, midsection unrestrained, hair unkempt and her face plain and unmade, and tells her she can't be a man. "Don't even try," Joan says. "Be a woman. It's powerful business when done correctly."

In the years since I left Wyoming, first for Colorado then back to New York for more graduate school, I have been moving toward an understanding of the ways my relationship to my body is entangled with my relationship to all the spaces I move through and the beings I move among, and even to the spaces and beings I will never encounter directly, and to the violence I was born into and raised inside, by which I mean this settler colonial project constructed by white supremacist logics on this land that was never supposed to be property.

But it would be so easy to surrender this understanding—to engulf myself fully in concerns with the appearance, ability, and longevity of my body. In the morning over coffee, I could scroll through images of fitness models and aptly named fitness influencers. I could, after working, go to the gym and carve away at my body in the ways that the fitness models and influencers showed me. Then, I could spend the evening logging each serving of food that I ate into an application on my iPhone made for tracking such things as calories and fats and carbs and protein. Before bed, I could lather myself in products that promise to aid in my fight against ugliness and aging. I could do all this scrubbing, smoothing, lathering in the name of self-care, and if I wanted to, I could spend all of my money on it. I could go deeply into debt in the name of health and beauty.

This surrender would be easy because it is programmed in my being. I know how to categorize foods as "good" and "bad." I know how to use exercise as both confession and repentance. I know how to confuse sweat for sanctity. And of course, measuring myself against a smaller and prettier and younger version of myself, even if that version is mythology, feels nearly as natural and involuntary as breathing.

Sometimes, even still, I get caught up in remembering the beauty of the running body. By "the beauty of the running body," I mean to say it was beautiful to me. I would catch glimpses of it—in the rearview mirror, reflecting back from sunglasses and windows and dark computer screens—and I'd feel the way I knew I was supposed to feel when staring into the ocean or gazing at pieces of important art or walking through the fossil halls at the American Museum of Natural History. When I looked at those things, I felt nothing. Nothing like what I felt looking at the running body. My face was hardened and hollowed, and I thought it was so pretty. It felt so separate from me, out of reach.

In *On Beauty and Being Just*, Elaine Scarry writes about the ways beauty is "a contagion of imitation." Many dislike this about beauty—argue that it's too dangerous, too violent—but Scarry defends beauty's knack for inspiring reproduction—generating a sense of longing for what we see. "When the eye sees someone beautiful, the whole body wants to reproduce the person," she writes. I often see it both ways: beauty as violent and dangerous; beauty as generative and necessary.

When I come across pictures of the running body, do I want to reproduce it? And if I do, what might this want offer? When I come across pictures of the running body, I can't help but notice how lovely being that way made me. How striking. I thought it was so beautiful how you could tell just by looking at my body that it was made to do the very thing it was doing. I think, even then, I could feel the danger in the beauty—but the trouble with danger is that it is thrilling.

In pictures of the running body taken after meets and at

parties and while hanging out with Melissa, Juli, and Olivia in our apartment, in pictures where I am relaxed and smiling, my hollowed face is glowing. That's why, in the years after, I started smiling with closed teeth. I thought it better camouflaged my filled-back-up cheeks.

I've heard people argue that analyzing beauty—looking at it closely, breaking it down for parts, trying to see what might be beneath—destroys it. Sometimes, I worry that's what I'm doing (to the running body, the running) with this writing. Sometimes, I think destroying is exactly what I should be doing.

Now, I'll admit I find the notion of beauty confusing. Or rather, I find its contradictions troubling. When I try to consider beauty—to work out what it means, how it works, when and how it is violent and when and how it is of good use—I feel a sense of suspension. I don't know if I'm up for the task. In response, I've turned to embrace the ugly and abject, the incomplete and messy, the soft and tender. But back then, my understanding of beauty was not complicated or contradictory. Beauty, to me, was the reflection of discipline from the inside to the outside of the body. I saw no problems with this way of thinking.

Beauty, or at least what often counts as beauty, is often the external representation of an internalization of what bell hooks calls the imperialist capitalist white supremacist patriarchy. Knowing this, I still have not reasoned myself all the way out of finding beauty in the most disciplined bodies. What I mean is: I have not shaken the notion that the way something *looks* often means something about the way that something *is*, i.e., that the faster a runner looks, the faster that runner must be. The faster and harder I became, the more I seemed to internalize the logic that if the composition of my body determines what I can do with it, and what I can do with my body determines my identity, then the composition of my body determines my identity. How do I unknow and unfeel that sense of satisfaction that came from, finally, feeling as if I had proof of something? What is beauty without the belief that what we see means something?

After neither our men's nor women's teams competed well at an early-season cross country meet in 2013, Rick told everyone to gather around him and listen up. My pubic bone was broken, had been broken for months, and from my place on the outside of the stretching circle, I limped in closer.

"It's obvious we aren't a national caliber team," he said. "Just do the eyeball test." He did not explain what he meant by "the eyeball test" because he did not need to. Most of my teammates looked down at the ground, some of them straight-ahead, some of them directly at Rick. I looked around. I counted the number of my teammates who passed "the eyeball test." Then, I counted the number of my teammates who I either knew or suspected were denying themselves food—who were going hungry. The second number was higher than the first. No one denied or refuted what Rick said, though I'm sure at least a few of us were thinking, *Someone should say something.*

A reminder: Two years before, during Juli and my sophomore season of cross country—the season that came after that summer, the season she started breaking records and I started breaking—our running bodies and the performances they achieved were held up by our coaches as examples for the rest of the team. It was never: "Look more like them." It was subtler, more difficult to trace. My coaches became two of the only men I knew who didn't say anything to me in concern about my body. Instead, they raised my scholarship to full tuition plus books plus an off-campus housing stipend that covered rent and groceries. I hoarded this stipend away and, after I could no longer compete, it got me through months of my low-paid internship in New York City.

At the end of the first cross country season after that summer, when our coaches awarded me with "Most Improved Runner" and Juli with MVP, they treated us both like we mattered more than the rest of our team. To them, our bodies (and so we) were worth something. Shortly after that season habits of disordered eating and overtraining began spreading through both the women's and men's teams. It becomes hard, here, to avoid causality.

When I was one of the fastest runners on the team I was, quite obviously, one of Rick's highest priorities. Once the fractures began and did not end, I was tossed aside. I went from feeling very close to Rick, as close as I was to my high school coaches, to rejection. It happened quickly. Out of a sense of guilt and duty, when I could no longer race or practice, I began volunteering in the athletic department. I updated our website, sent out newsletters to alumni, answered phones. I had multiple redshirts available to me and I was nowhere near out of eligibility. Even now, I can't understand why anyone allowed me to think I had to earn my keep in this way. During this time, my guilt and shame felt unending, but I can't help but wonder how simple it might have been to relieve.

When a runner breaks after visible decreases in body, the judgment and blame falls on them exclusively. At least, this is the only way I experienced and saw and heard of it happening: Unless it happens across a team at a very high frequency, making it impossible to ignore, the coaches and trainers and people in positions of power and authority over the young athlete are held to no responsibility. It's so normalized to blame the athlete that even the athletes blame the athlete.

At races, I might have seen a runner I hadn't seen since last season and I might have leaned over to one of my teammates with wide and knowing eyes and said, "Look." And my teammate might have followed my gaze and agreed, "Oh my gosh. She got so lean." Once she turned up on the injury list, if she turned up on the injury list, someone might have thought or said something about how she took what was called "the shortcut." For elite runners, it is acceptable and expected to lean out over a number of years, but doing so too quickly—getting too hungry—is looked down on. Though, of course, only when it ends in a series of career-ending injuries.

After I took the shortcut but before my bones began fracturing, I heard a runner talking to her coach after a meet. The runner was one of the best in our conference, and it was widely known that she had an eating disorder. People on my team would recall looking over at her before the start of races and seeing patches of fur all over her face and body. She was often injured, but even when she recovered and started racing again, she still appeared dangerously lean. "Remember last summer?" the coach asked the runner. "Yes," she said, "I got so lean—all I ate was fruit!" They smiled and exchanged high-fives. As I looked and listened on, even though I had done nearly the same thing as she, I felt a strange mix of envy and pity.

When I was in the NCAA, disordered eating spread through teams quickly. You could watch it happen throughout a season. You could look across the starting line from week to week and watch it spread from teammate to teammate, then from team to team. The destruction of bodies was the primary narrative of collegiate women's cross country.

Juli and I used to spend many of our phone conversations trying to wrap our heads around what happened, what was happening.

"I saw people who were better than me, or who looked the way I thought I was supposed to look, or were doing something I thought I was supposed to do, and I tried to find out everything about what they did then do it."

"I think that's what I did with you. I started running the miles you were running, eating the things you were eating."

"Maybe if we would have seen people doing the right things, we wouldn't have done what we did to our bodies."

"Maybe."

We discussed how Annie, who graduated after our freshman year, would often say things like, "Everything in moderation—

even moderation," anytime anyone on the team would stress over a slice of pizza or bowl of ice cream. Though she was one of my favorite people to run with, and I loved looking out ahead during track workouts and tempos and mile repeats and seeing her stride and thinking maybe one day that could be me, I remember feeling relief that she graduated and left Athens before I stopped eating. If she were there, I presumed she would have said something to both me and Juli. I figured she would have tried to intervene.

Sometimes, and much more often now than when I was still running, the culture of elite and collegiate running is forced to take responsibility for its breaking bodies. This happened in 2018 when Greg Metcalf, the head distance coach at the University of Washington, stepped down after allegations surfaced that he had produced and perpetuated eating disorders and other mental health concerns (depression, fear, anxiety) across both his men's and women's teams. It was no surprise to hear and read about what the University of Washington distance runners dealt with—it was only surprising that someone was being held responsible. From what I heard from Juli (who is much more plugged into these conversations than me) and what I read online, the athletic department was made aware of Metcalf's tendencies as early as 2015. Tendencies such as calling one of his male runners a "fat piece of shit" because, he says, he thought the runner could handle it, and anyway, that's how he was spoken to as an athlete. "I know Greg. He's a very charismatic man. He has some serious personal issues that spilled over into his professional life. What is being reported in the media is just the tip of the iceberg," one of the message board posts read.

Over the phone, I can't remember if it was Juli or I who asked the other, "Can you imagine if every coach who perpetuated disordered eating was forced to step down?" We laughed grimly, knowing there would hardly be any coaches left.

It is always the tip of the iceberg. Afterall, disordered eating is perpetuated by Western culture writ large, and its presence is made more prominent within the culture of elite athletics. Like nearly everything else inside our neoliberal regime, disordered eating is normalized as an individual problem. And further, it is only seen as a problem in the first place if the person who cannot eat or who cannot stop eating inhabits a body that exists outside the bounds of normativity. It goes without saying (though I can't help saying it anyway) that reality shows like *The Biggest Loser* and *My 600-lb Life* thrive under this logic—as does, of course, the gargantuan health, beauty, diet, and fitness industry. Like all industry within capitalism, this one feeds on (then exploits) our collective shame—makes us feel like it is our shame, as individuals, that we must fix on our own (by, of course, buying more things).

It feels as if there is an assumption that in order to have any shot of living up to a standard of health—which is really a standard of appearance (body size, weight, shape)—which are really standards of beauty and ability that have been constructed by centuries of white supremacy and heteronormativity—one must engage in a battle against hunger, rest, flesh. This assumption exists inside competitive sport to an even higher degree, though it sometimes hides under layers of veiling. The stakes, in sport, are understood as higher—you must be more healthy *and* you must be more disciplined. The result, in my experience, was the sense that disordered eating would be an inevitability. It was never some head-scratcher when a body disappeared off a starting line and a name off a roster. I suppose I just never thought I would be the one who disappeared—or maybe I knew that disappearance was a possibility? (A question to which I cannot stop returning.)

The rhetoric of sport is one of boundaries and limits—or, more precisely, transcending boundaries and pushing past limits. It's mind over matter. It's just do it. It's pain is weakness leaving the body. It's sink or swim, but you better not sink. It's you were born for this and this is your destiny and you can be better than everyone else as long as you're willing to bleed.

When we were in high school, someone from the local running shoe company interviewed Penny and me after a meet. When the interviewer asked what advice I would give to other high school runners wanting to get faster I said, without hesitating, "You just have to work harder than you think you can."

In the days after Juli and I talked about Metcalf's resignation, I often caught myself wondering how fast I could have been if Rick were as abusive as Metcalf. How far would I have gone to prove my worth to him? Would I have reached a higher rung before I fell off the ladder? If I was always going to fall anyway, would getting even one rung higher have made me feel more whole, less hole-y? There is a certain ease in sliding back into questions like these.

Now, when I see professional and collegiate runners toeing starting lines, I cannot help but see all the phantoms in their shadows. The bones that got broke, the runners who broke themselves. How many runners must lay their dreams to rest in order to save their lives? I could not survive the running body. But what is that law about energy?

In Laramie, I saw two ghosts regularly. I saw them at the gym and grocery store. Coffee shops and sidewalks. I saw them walking into the same bars I was walking out of. The first often smiled at me. Our eyes would always meet. The second seemed spooked each time our paths crossed. I think she saw me and my body as cautionary.

"Did you know that anorexic girl from the gym has a boyfriend? They were here together before you walked in," a friend remarked one night coolly.

"She used to be a runner," I said, trying to seem distracted by something on my phone.

When she asked me how I knew, I didn't tell her about the ghosts or the hauntings. How when we look at each other, we see our past (but not passed) bodies. I don't tell her sometimes I feel like Jecky—the ghost who lived in my grandparent's house—waiting for a flood to put out the burning.

# VI.

ATHLETES OFTEN LEARN to deny reality for the well-being of their ambitions, which are anchored, of course, in dreams, which are anchored, of course, in delusion—in fantasy. For most athletes, they have to be. Perhaps I should speak less generally. How might I have stopped my dreams from eating away at my body?

As an athlete I relied on the disavowal of uncertainty. I must have trained myself into believing I could control everything, especially my body. This must be one of the reasons why I fell so hard in love with running—for a good long while, I largely *was* in control, or at least, it felt that way. The harder I worked, the faster I ran. I must have thought I had the power. But I must have known, in the way that knowing is feeling and feeling is knowing, that running so many miles over so many months on empty would break down my body. I must have ignored the knowing. I must have turned myself into a fool, the way that all lovers do.

But now I am left with this flesh. My months are no longer marked with the certainty of starts and finishes. Now I must try to unlearn everything—this false system of beliefs I beat into myself over every mile, every stride. Out on the roads, I defied my body until it felt new and then I told myself this is The Real You. On the cross country course and out on the track, I tried and tried to make my body a house for pain, a place where the pain might feel welcome, might stay. I thought it was the right thing to do—to work harder then harder then harder, and to discipline away all the parts of me that wanted to stop or quit or take a break—and I thought if I did all the things I thought were right, I would be all right too.

On the course, the runner must believe in the silliest, most superfluous of things. In heroism and immortality and victory. In whatever comes after, the once-runner struggles to believe in anything. The body cannot be controlled, and because it cannot be controlled, it is unforgivable. The mind is destructive. It was supposed to be the thing that got you your dreams but instead it destroyed your body. The self is untrustworthy. The habit is no good, but no matter, it's still got you hooked. All the old routines are nothing more than proof of your dependency, your instability. Without them you feel purposeless and empty. With them you are self-destructive and crazy. Some days it feels like the only thing left to do is throw your whole self into healing, letting go, or at least, loosening. Other days it feels like the only thing left to do is to keep trying, by which I mean: to lace up your old shoes and match your cadence to the rhythm of maybe maybe maybe.

I think it's that rhythm and that maybe that hooked me from the beginning—traveling to middle-school meets across the county, legs stuck to brown-leather bus seats, fantasizing about how fast I could be, always pushing to an end I couldn't see.

During the first fracturing I spent hours a day in the pool—often two but sometimes up to four—alternating between swimming laps and water running. Legs churning water in the deep end, I would ask my future self, the healed one, *How does it feel to be here, mixing it up for the first time with the top runners in the country?* Then, I'd whisper the words under my breath, "I'm just so grateful that I came out on the other side of my injuries and that I'm able to be here doing this. I'm so lucky to have so many supportive people who believed in me even when I didn't believe in myself. I've dreamed of this moment one hundred times and it feels amazing that it's happening."

But believing in something does not make it true. Will not make it happen, or will not undo its happening. Does not thrust it (the something) into the real. Soon, my body could no longer hold itself up to my magical thinking. I lost faith. It happened quickly.

People say failure is good because it teaches you. And this is true. I can't say that it's not. I have learned. But what people say less is this. I would give back all this failure, all this learning, to watch an arm raise a pistol toward the sky, to feel that buzz move itself up legs to chest, hear the shot, feel the running body take off, begin to make its meaning, step for step to the rhythm of hard, controlled breathing. I would unlearn every lesson failure taught me for a chance to vanish again into the running.

IT'S SUMMER AGAIN and I'm spending time with my family in West Virginia. It's impossible for me, when I'm here, not to feel overwhelmed with the yearning to go running.

I'm out a few miles away from my great-grandparents' farmhouse in Preston County. They're not alive anymore, and haven't been since I was a kid, but you can still smell their skin in the living room, see the imprints of their bodies on the furniture. With each labored breath, I try to take pleasure in the gently rolling hills. This road, Limestone, climbs up and down over ridges and valleys that have not yet been ruined. Once I turn around, I know I only have about a mile or so until the long decline I enjoyed on the way out becomes an incline—just as long and ten times as cruel, unrelenting. When I reach the bottom of the climb, which my family calls The Knob, I slow and inhale deeply, but the breath cannot reach. It's the kind of hill that would have been no match for the running body: slow-burning, a thrill to see how long the land keeps climbing, knowing the peak will mean a hit of affirmation and endorphins that will propel the body forward even faster than it was already going. I press onto my toes, shorten my stride, and keep my arms punching punching punching through thick humidity. This is how my dad taught me. The strain of the steep grade gets to me early. I tell my body to hang on and that it's just pain and pain always ends if you can get to the other side, but rhetoric like this no longer works on me the way long, increasingly steep grades work on me. I'm trying to communicate with the body in a language it no longer understands.

When I stop, seconds later, it feels as if my body has disobeyed my mind, but I know now that my mind and body are not separate things. I stand, both bewildered and relieved, on the edge of the slanted asphalt, then I begin walking. After a few minutes my heartbeat slows and I see the top of the hill. I run the rest of the way up, then keep running. There's one small crest left between the old farmhouse and the old red barn and the handful of headstones marking our family's dead. I see my dad sitting on the old porch. I hear the swing squeaking. He hollers out to me, says my breathing was so loud he could hear me for a longtime coming.

I often feel as if I am either running or not running—it's a binary that threatens to keep me from ever just being.

One night, back before flood, my grandpa says he was sitting at the kitchen table when he noticed the back door was left wide open, and so he got up to close it, and he did close it, he says, but a short time later, he noticed the door came open again, and so he got up to close it again, and he did close it again. This time he even locked it. "And I'll be damned," he says when he tells the story now, "that damned old door came open again." Instead of getting up a third time, he just said, "Okay Jecky. Close it when you're done."

Recently Juli told me she hopes that someday running will become therapeutic for her. She said, "Maybe I'll just heal magically."

I think of it as a kind of haunting. How my pubic bone, years after fracturing, buzzes with, not pain exactly, but a memory of pain. How I feel the shock of the pain-memory spreading from the site of the fracture to the rest of my body.

Ask for forgiveness, not permission goes the saying. I never asked either of my body. I should say sorry. I should say I didn't mean to. I only wanted to move forward at a faster rate. I wasn't trying to break parts of you. I only wanted to destroy as much of you as I needed to in order to run faster and farther without stopping. And I should promise to never wreak such harmful havoc on my body again. But what if my body suspects I am lying? It's true that many things only happen once, but what about all the things that happen more than that?

I no longer remember how it feels to feel so much for the thing: One foot in front of the other, faster, longer, smoother, and now you're floating, and now it's easy. According to neuroscience, the more you try to remember something, the more you forget it. I wonder if there is a similar relationship between language and the body. The more precisely you try to capture a feeling, the further it slips from your grasp.

In *The Chronology of Water*, Lidia Yuknavitch writes, "Language is a metaphor for experience. It's as arbitrary as the mass of chaotic images we call memory—but we can put it into lines to narrativize over fear." This is how I tell you, back there, I believed that if I could make narrative sense of what happened—what I did to my body and why and what the costs ended up being—then I could reach the end of this story. And I thought if I could reach the end of this story, I could reach the end of my grief. Perhaps it has been a mistake to put faith in clarity. In the linear. In the before and after. Beginnings, middles, endings. Nothing I've let go of has claw marks on it because I've never let go.

Sometimes I crave the earth. I feel an urgent need to find a spot of ground on which to lie down. I must feel it breathe. I must look up at the sky and pay very close attention to the way the clouds are moving.

Sometimes remembering—no, feeling—that none of this belongs to me feels like a kind of healing. A gentle kind, I think. Because it's inside that system of thinking that I care both less and more about my body.

Ever since I was in my early-twenties I have often, no matter where I am, felt the need to pack up and flee. I often follow these needs. I keep moving. But from time to time I slow down to worry if I am experiencing a need to flee my body, rather than a need to flee whatever person or place onto which I am projecting the need.

"Where is there a place for you to be?" asks Hazel Motes, the haunted preacher in Flannery O'Connor's *Wise Blood*. "No place," he answers, "In yourself right now is all the place you've got." It was July of my first summer in Laramie when I read *Wise Blood*. Shortly after, I got a simple house tattooed on the top of my left wrist. Triangular roof, rectangular foundation, and walls. I had been drawing the image on myself for weeks. I didn't yet know what it meant, I only knew that I wanted to make it permanent.

What if, anyway, the story of your life is contained in the days lost—not tucked—away? The days that pass quietly, though not suddenly—not too fast or too slow, actually. When the snow falls slow and slanted into the February gray. When, for just a moment, the way it's falling feels like a metaphor for grief when grief is on its way to becoming something other than grief. When the feeling passes without consequence. And you, it seems, only got out of bed to get back in. Nestling, eventually, back into the stale warmth of your own dreams.

Or what if your most important days are the days in which you feel small, brief, fleeting?

Or what if your best days are the ones in which you feel less like a person and more like a molecule of haze?

What if even the happiest people want to change their lives, stories, bodies?

There exists a German word, *sehnsucht*, that cannot be translated to English. *Sehnsucht* signifies a sensation of longing for what cannot be expressed. Inexpressible longing. And then there is the Welsh, *hwyl*, which means something like spirit longing. But what is spirit? Do the Welsh know? Can they tell me? I feel as if I long for something very specific, and nameless, and floating.

Throughout high school and college, when I spent my summers teaching small children to float, I'd place my hands on their backs and drag them through the water until their bodies turned weightless and horizontal in the shallow end. "Don't let me go," they would beg. "I won't," I would promise. I'd wait for the rise and fall of their chest to steady, then I'd quickly remove my hands from their bodies. They would float perfectly for entire instants until recognizing the absence of my skin on theirs. Then, they would shriek, bend their torsos, and be pulled underneath. Half a second later, I'd pull their bodies back up, hold them very tightly and say, over and over again, "You were floating, you were floating." I don't know if they ever believed me.

Sometimes, on cross country courses, the starting line and finish line are far from one another, and so when the racers are standing on the starting line they can't see the finish line, and when the racers have crossed the finish line they cannot look back to the place from which they came before they heard the gun, saw the smoke, began running. Cross country, then, requires a certain degree of faith. But when races take place on the 400-meter oval of the track, the starting and finish lines are always in view. And for most races, the starting line is the same as the finish line. The line does not change but the meaning does. And so, on the track, with each lap, the runners move across the line and across the line and across the line. Then, the bell rings. The bell means that the line will now signify an ending.

Without the bells and the lines and the ringing, everything feels more like ceaseless spinning. I imagine a merry-go-round. I imagine myself on the platform, the surroundings blurry. It's not operated by any sort of machine. It is operated by me. I have to, occasionally, jump off the platform and wrap my hands tight around the paint-chipped metal. Cool to the touch. Then I have to start running. The harder I run, the faster the spin will become, the longer it will last. Individual trees become collectives of green. I experience a kind of joy in going dizzy.

That summer, the running body consumed flesh and bone, and it consumed me. It ate and ate until all that was left would serve its need for distance and speed. At least, that's one way to tell the story. Like I can unhinge then and now, before and after. Like I disappeared and the running body is what replaced me.

Another way: I cannot separate the running body from me, the happened from the happening. Does everything end or does nothing?

Has every sentence only made more mess? The closer I try to get to the center of what happened, the clearer I try to see, the more I begin to think the center is missing. In its place is an opening. A place with no language, no ending. I miss running.

Before Grandma Sue got diagnosed with lung cancer and quit smoking, my sister made a habit of taking whole packs of Winston Lights out of her purse and throwing them in the trash. I imagine my grandma now, walking around her house from wastebasket to wastebasket, digging her smokes out.

From my desk one day I watched a girl running from something I could not see. I leaned closer and closer to her body until my forehead rested on the dirty glass and my breath made it foggy. I pulled my head slightly back and caught my reflection; I watched my eyes watch her run. My body felt heavy. A rush of jealousy turned me hot. The girl moved as if the ground wasn't concerning. Her legs and torso like a wave that built and built without crashing. Forward, forward, forward only. Ponytail suspended in air like daydreams. I realized she was not being chased or chasing. I realized she was laughing. I realized she was just running. Just running and just running and just running and I no longer remember how that feels: I only remember that it *felt*. A friend recently told me she felt something in her bones, and I knew she was lying. The only thing you can feel in your bones is breaking. The girl could not feel her bones. Inside them, nothing bad was happening. Inside her mind, she was not yet calculating. Calories, mistakes, the people she'll never be, the bodies she'll never see when she looks in the mirror and sees her body.

From my desk, I noticed the girl was gone or was never there or it was months ago that she ran by—the grass a late-spring green, or dead from wintering.

From my desk, the girl never stops running.

But today I am sitting on the front porch that once belonged to my Great-Grandpa Walt and Great-Grandma Annie. I am sitting on the newest of the old porch swings, and it's swaying a bit here and there, but only defiantly and with much to say about it, the creaks chiming in with the occasional sound of a cow or bird or the rare truck passing. The sky in front of me, directly, hanging over the red barn, is a light and pure blue that reminds me of nothing. Its blue is singular and self-evident. In its midst, the clouds seem lazy and noncommittal; unsure of what they are to do. But to the left the sky is different. It's covered in clouds of certainty, steel-colored and steely. The gravestones resting beneath all those clouds look unsettling, though quite settled, I'm sure. The three flies making meaning out of their lives by buzzing will be dead soon, probably, and so I do nothing to bother their buzzing. No shooing.

There is a storm, as they say, brewing. I smell the rain moving toward the old farmhouse and this old porch swing and me. It's faint. The birds are ad-libbing. They're the kind of flock that doesn't bother with harmony, but there's something decent in their disorganized cacophony; I'm listening.

I left for a moment and just returned and the sky has changed. It's now blue and blue and blue—the whole thing. To the left, right, straight-ahead, and probably also behind, though I can't see it and can't be sure. The rain never came. The birds have stopped their singing and the flies have stopped their buzzing, and I wonder what they're all doing now, instead of making sound.

The hint of moisture hanging still in the air seems stale now—a vestige announcing the absence of sprinkle, drizzle, downpouring. I imagine the difference the rain would have made. The smell of hot, wet asphalt. The steam dancing. Humidity moving in waves, taking up occupancy. The would-be relief of the clouds' release. How, once fallen, all those drops of rain could have become different things, though always, without fail, of the same properties.

# NOTES & REFERENCES

**Section I.**

The reference to Narcissus comes from Edith Hamilton's *Mythology: Timeless Tales of Gods and Heroes* (Little, Brown and Company, 1942), a text that was assigned as summer reading for Mrs. DiPasquale's AP English Literature and Composition course.

*Once a Runner* by John L. Parker Jr. was first published in 1978 by Cedarwinds, then republished in 2010 by Scribner. The book and its protagonist, Quenton Cassidy, have acquired a cult-like following amongst track athletes.

*Running with the Buffaloes: A Season Inside with Mark Wetmore, Adam Goucher, and the University of Colorado Men's Cross Country Team* by Chris Lear was originally published by Trafford Publishing in 2000 and re-released in 2011 by Lyons Press. Like *Once a Runner*, Lear's *Running with the Buffaloes* has a cult-like following.

*The Electric Kool-Aid Acid Test* by Tom Wolfe was published in 1968 by Farrar, Straus and Giroux. I did not read it until 2012 or 2013, and when I did, I was frustrated by my inability to imagine how this text would have inspired Wetmore's coaching philosophy. Though, on pages 27-28 of *Running with the Buffaloes*, Lear explains how reading about Ken Kesey and the Merry Pranksters and their Acid Tests marked a turning point for him as a young man: "The hippies demonstrated to him the allure of living 'on the periphery of existence.' Wetmore took the lessons from their experiences and applied them to his coaching." This application involved Wetmore's athletes suffering as much as possible to see how good they could be, "safety be damned." And such a coaching philosophy does seem to resist the straight world (and its limits, its safety) that Kesey and the Merry Pranksters were also resisting or trying to resist. "I'd rather be a lightning rod than a seismograph," Kesey says.

On page 42 of *Running with the Buffaloes*, Lear details the way Adam Goucher never ate lunch. As Lear explains, "If he is hungry, he will have a granola bar or another light snack . . . He used to eat more . . . At the Olympic Trials in Atlanta in 1996, he weighed 145. After the 5,000-meter final, where he finished a disappointing fourteenth, Wetmore told him he was fat. Goucher was livid. When he calmed down he realized Wetmore was right, and he has made a conscious effort to lose any excess weight since then. He feels the difference . . . Still cut, he does not lift weights. 'I love to lift,' he says, but it bulks him up too much, so Wetmore will not allow it."

The video called "Eat a Dorito," featuring Kara and Adam

Goucher, was published by FloTrack in April 2007. In the later parts of the four-minute video, the interviewer asks Kara how she and Adam approach their diet now. "We do eat dessert," she explains, then laughs nervously and says her coach at Nike, Alberto Salazar, "should leave." Twelve years later, largely because of Kara Goucher's decision to speak out against her former coach, Salazar would be served a four-year ban from the United States Anti-Doping Agency. Soon after, another former Nike athlete, Mary Cain, would also speak out, in a video produced by the Opinion department at *The New York Times* called, "I Was the Fastest Girl in America, Until I Joined Nike." Cain details, amongst other things, how and why she developed an emotionally-damaging and injury-causing eating disorder while training under Salazar. Following Cain's video, Amy Yoder Begley, another former Nike athlete who trained under Salazar, would speak out against him on Twitter, writing, "After placing 6th in the 10,000m at the 2011 USATF championships, I was kicked out of the Oregon Project. I was told I was too fat and 'had the biggest butt on the starting line.'" In 2020, the United States Center for SafeSport would permanently ban Salazar from the sport for sexual and emotional misconduct. Cain would go on to sue Salazar and Nike for $20 million.

"How Megan Goethals Got Her Groove Back" by Rachel Sturtz was published in *Runner's World* in September of 2011, during my sophomore season of cross country at Ohio University.

The Dick's Sporting Goods spot is called "Gold in US," and it premiered during the 2016 Summer Olympics.

In this section, I reference Simone Weil's *Gravity and Grace* (translated by Arthur Wills, Bison Books, 1997). I was introduced to Weil and *Gravity and Grace*, which was first published in the United States in 1952, through Chris Kraus's *Aliens & Anorexia* (Semiotext(e), 2000). Both Weil and Kraus influenced my thinking and writing, and Weil's thinking, in particular, haunts the book, influencing my thinking about beauty and perfection in section three.

### Section II.

My question—"Can we control what we inherit, whether it be through the violence of culture or the violence of nature or the violence of culture on nature?"—was influenced by my readings in feminist science and technology studies, especially the work of Donna J. Haraway and Victoria Pitts-Taylor.

Joan Didion's line, "We tell ourselves stories in order to live," opens her essay, "The White Album." This line—so striking, so intuitively true—is often taken out of context. By "stories" I sense Didion means myths, as she goes on to explain: "We interpret what we see, select the most workable of the multiple choices. We live entirely, especially if we are writers, by the imposition of a narrative line upon disparate images, by the 'ideas' with which we have learned to freeze the shifting phantasmagoria which is our actual experience." Going on, Didion writes, "Or at least we do for a while. I am talking here about a time when I began to doubt the premises of all the stories I had ever told myself, a common condition but one I found troubling." I wrote the first drafts of this book under a similar condition.

This book's thinking about Plato, Gorgias, and the influence of the ancient Greeks were shaped by the Ancient Rhetorics course I took with Dr. Lois Agnew at Syracuse University during the fall of 2020. In this section and the next, I draw from Plato's *Gorgias*, translated by Benjamin Jowett and published by The Project Gutenberg.

I have primarily learned about the 1985 flood of Tucker County through listening to my grandparents' stories from that time.

In this section, I reference John Berger's *Ways of Seeing* (Penguin Books, 1990). *Ways of Seeing* became influential as looking and being looked at continued to emerge throughout my writing.

There are various local, national, and even international news stories about the young woman from Cincinnati who went missing in Grand Teton National Park in the summer of 2016. The details I included can be found in articles such as "Searchers for teen in Wyo. wilderness mystified when she's found with hair dyed, clothes changed" by Katie Mettler for *The Washington Post* (August 8, 2016) and "Missing teen found with altered appearance placed in protective custody" by Joanna Walters for *The Guardian* (August 7, 2016).

In this section, I reference Elisabeth Kübler-Ross's *On Death and Dying* (Simon & Schuster/ Touchstone, 1969). I found Kübler-Ross and her work through my research into "the five stages of grief," which I was aware of from popular culture but did not know its source.

The conversations with Juli included in this section were recorded with permission during July of 2016. I often think of (or thought of) Juli's and my experiences as similar; it felt important to understand the ways our stories, experiences, and perspectives differed. I wanted to listen to how Juli was, at the time, making sense of what we did to our bodies.

The Iowa State runner whose blog post I mention is named Dani Stack. Stack is now a counselor specializing in sports psychology, eating disorders, and substance use.

My consideration of athletics in ancient Greece was sparked by my reading of works such as David M. Pritchard's *Sport, Democracy and War in Classical Athens* (Cambridge University Press, 2013), Stephen G. Miller's *Ancient Greek Athletics* (Yale University Press, 2006), Debra Hawhee's *Bodily Arts: Rhetoric and Athletics in Ancient Greece* (University of Texas Press, 2004), and Ana Carden-Coyne's *Reconstructing the Body: Classicism, Modernism, and the First World War* (Oxford University Press, 2009).

**Section III.**
The note about physical pain being the "only antidote I thought I'd ever need to all my tired metaphysical suffering" was inspired by my coming across a similar sentiment from Karl Marx.

My consideration of the chemical process of falling and being in love was sparked by a student's research (at Arapahoe Community College in Littleton, Colorado) on the use of MDMA in couples therapy.

I mention Bessel van der Kolk's *The Body Keeps the Score: Brain, Mind, and Body in the Healing of Trauma* (Penguin, 2014). Though I had not and still have not finished reading this text, I am intrigued by its argument and the ways it has circulated through popular culture.

My considerations of the way "Plato and his posse" thought about hunger and its entanglements with pleasure and pain come from an exchange between Socrates and Callicles in Plato's *Gorgias* dialogue.

The quote from Chris comes from a blog he wrote that was posted on his sponsor's website. In this section, I paraphrase part of his post from memory, but the actual quote reads: "You see, I'm not really supposed to be here. I shouldn't actually still be doing this. College walk-ons don't finish top-10 in World Major Marathons. I feel like I've already won the running lottery, and that allows me to race with such freedom."

### Section IV.

Allie Ostrander, whose body the commentators discussed as "very thin" and "underdeveloped" at the 2016 Olympic Track and Field Trials, ended her professional contract in 2021 to, as she explained, focus on her mental and physical health. This announcement came six months after Ostrander announced that she had entered partial hospitalization for eating disorder recovery, then days later, competed in the 2021 Olympic Track and Field Trials.

My writing in this section about anti-diet movements comes

from the work of Christy Harrison—her podcast *Food Psych* and book *Anti-Diet: Reclaim Your Time, Money, Well-Being, and Happiness Through Intuitive Eating* (Little Brown, Spark, 2019). Reflections on whiteness and the connections across racism, classism, healthism, ableism, body size discrimination, and homophobia were influenced by texts such as Nell Irvin Painter's *The History of White People* (W.W. Norton and Company, 2011), Sabrina Strings's *Fearing the Black Body: The Racial Origins of Fat Phobia* (New York University Press, 2019), Angela Y. Davis's *Women, Race & Class* (Vintage Books, 1983), Kiese Laymon's *Heavy: An American Memoir* (Scribner, 2019), and Tressie McMillan Cottom's *Thick: And Other Essays* (The New Press, 2019).

**Section V.**

My articulation of desire, longing, objectification, and subjectification in this section was undoubtedly influenced by my reading of Roland Barthes's *A Lover's Discourse*.

My thinking about causality in this section was influenced by Emerson Whitney's writing about causality and transness in *Heaven* (McSweeney's, 2021).

My considerations of the connections across beauty, oppression, and capitalism in this section and throughout the text were guided by my reading in feminist theory and texts such as Naomi Wolf's *The Beauty Myth: How Images of Beauty Are Used Against Women* (Harper Perennial, 2002).

My reflections on entanglement and interdependency have been influenced by a range of writers and theorists such as Karen Barad, Robin Wall Kimmerer, Wendell Berry, Kathleen Stewart, Heather Davis, Zoe Todd, Kim TallBear, and Annemarie Mol.

In my consideration of beauty in this section, I reference Elaine Scarry's *On Beauty and Being Just* (Princeton University Press, 2001). My writing in this section was also influenced by Susan Bordo's *Unbearable Weight: Feminism, Western Culture, and the Body* (University of California Press, 1992), and the first place I came across bell hooks's formulation of the "imperialist capitalist white supremacist patriarchy" was in *Teaching to Transgress: Education as the Practice of Freedom* (Routledge, 1994).

Many of my details regarding the firing of and allegations against Greg Metcalf were drawn from personal conversations and "Inside The Allegations Against Former UW Track Coach" by Eilís O'Neill for WBUR (August 3, 2018).

My writing about sport culture in this section and throughout the book was sharpened by my reading of *So Many Olympic Exertions* by Anelise Chen (Kaya Press, 2017).

**Section VI.**
In this section I quote from Lidia Yuknavitch's *The Chronology of Water* (Hawthorne Books, 2011).

The line about claw marks alludes to a line from David Foster Wallace's *Infinite Jest*: "Everything I've ever let go of has claw marks on it." I read *Infinite Jest* (Little, Brown and Company, 1996) in 2015 and was influenced by Foster's treatment of sport, addiction, and recovery.

I also draw, in this section, from Flannery O'Connor's *Wise Blood*—I came across *Three by Flannery O'Connor* (Signet, 1983) at the University of Wyoming library and read *Wise Blood* in one sitting, fully transfixed by Hazel Motes, having no clue (somehow) that it was a classic.

My sense of a center that is missing alludes to similar language from Joan Didion in *Slouching Towards Bethlehem* (Farrar, Straus and Giroux, 2008), which Didion draws from W.B. Yeats's poem "The Second Coming."

# ACKNOWLEDGMENTS

Thank you, first, to my mother—the first runner I knew. I suppose I wanted to know where you went and what became of you when you took off down the road. Thank you to my father, who sparked and stoked my love for sport, competition, and testing oneself. Thank you both for your love and support and encouragement and belief. For supplying the desk. Thank you to Molly and Isaac. Thank you to my grandparents, Denny and Jane, for sharing your stories. Thank you to my grandmother, Sue, for teaching me so much in such a brief amount of time.

Thank you to my writing teachers—especially Sarah Green, Sarah Einstein, and Kelly K. Ferguson at Ohio University and Beth Loffreda, Rattawut Lapcharoensap, Frieda Knobloch, and Andy Fitch at the University of Wyoming. Thank you, especially, to Beth and Rattawut, for all the ways you nurtured and challenged and shaped the drafts that became this book. Thank you to my students—who have also been the teachers.

Thank you to the MFA program in Creative Writing at the University of Wyoming—for providing the space, funding, and community.

Thank you to my classmates, friends, and workshop group. Let's meet at Front Street—or better yet, The Buck. Love and gratitude especially to Kat, Liz, Maria, Lilly, Alec, Ammon, Trey, Kristine, Bryce, Carly, Kristi, and Bethann.

Thank you to my teammates and coaches—especially Jeff Kline, John Bender, Penny, Juli, Melissa, and Olivia. Thank you to Melissa and Olivia for reading earlier versions of the manuscript and sharing your thoughtful and heartfelt responses.

Thank you to Steve Almond for choosing *The Running Body* and to Christine Stroud and Mike Good at Autumn House Press for bringing it to life. Thank you to *The Fiddlehead* for publishing an essay excerpted from this book, "The Mirror Cannot Be True, and Yet I Cannot Stop Looking," in their Spring 2020 issue. Thank you especially to *The Fiddlehead's* creative nonfiction editor Alicia Elliot, who reignited my belief in this work during a time when the flame threatened to burn out.

Thank you, Joey—for sharing so much, for teaching me about the most important things, for your partnership, for your sense of humor and play and tenderness. Thank you, especially, for sharing your family, all of whom have expanded my heart.

I have run these miles and written these words on the stolen and occupied native land of the Cheyenne, Eastern Shoshone, Arapaho, Ute, Oceti Sakowin, Massawomeck, Osage, Shawnee, Kaskaskia, Hopewell, Adena, Myaamia, and Haudenosaunee peoples. Though inadequate, I offer my gratitude to the land and its stewards.

# NEW & FORTHCOMING RELEASES

*Seed Celestial* by Sara R. Burnett
**2021 Autumn House Poetry Prize | selected by Eileen Myles**

*Bittering the Wound* by Jacqui Germain
**2021 CAAPP Book Prize | selected by Douglas Kearney**

*The Running Body* by Emily Pifer
**2021 Autumn House Nonfiction Prize | selected by Steve Almond**

*Entry Level* by Wendy Wimmer
**2021 Autumn House Fiction Prize | selected by Deesha Philyaw**

*The Scorpion's Question Mark* by J. D. Debris
**2022 Donald Justice Poetry Prize | selected by Cornelius Eady**

*Given* by Liza Katz Duncan
**2022 Rising Writer Prize in Poetry | selected by Donika Kelly**

*Ishmael Mask* by Charles Kell

*Origami Dogs* by Noley Reid

*For our full catalog please visit autumnhouse.org*